Your Guide to the CFP® CERTIFICATION EXAM

Matthew Brandeburg, CFP®

A Supplement to Financial Planning Coursework and Self-Study Materials

ISBN: 1449998321
ISBN-13: 9781449998325

CONTENTS

Part I:

WHAT TO EXPECT ON THE CFP®
CERTIFICATION EXAM

HOW MUCH SHOULD YOU STUDY?

Because there will be so much material presented to you, it's important to know how many hours you should study in order to be prepared for the exam. With a national pass rate just over 50 percent, the CFP® Certification Exam requires a high level of organization, and a carefully thought out plan if you want to pass. Your plan must begin with an understanding that you'll probably never reach the point where you feel like you've mastered the material completely. However, if you study the right number of hours, you'll know you're as prepared as possible.

The leading CFP® review providers recommend you spend the following number of hours preparing for the exam:

Review Provider	Recommended Hours of Study
College for Financial Planning	200 to 250 hours
Dalton	200 hours
Kaplan	200 hours before live review class
Keir	200 to 300 hours
Ken Zahn	140 hours before live review class

I recommend studying three hundred hours and completing five thousand multiple choice questions before attempting the exam.

HOW TO PREPARE FOR THE EXAM

The most productive way to prepare for the CFP® Certification Exam is to complete as many practice questions as possible. This allows you to see which types of questions you're likely to face on the exam, and lets you learn from your mistakes. It's okay if you find yourself doing the same questions every few weeks, as long as your approach to answering the questions is still strong. In other words, if you're simply memorizing answers it's not a good use of your time. As a general rule, you should attempt one thousand practice questions before cycling back to previous questions you've already attempted. For any practice test or quiz that you take, be sure to record your scores on the summary sheets provided (see Appendix: Blank Worksheets). Tracking your progress is essential.

During the first few weeks you're studying for the exam, it's common to score between 50 percent and 70 percent on practice tests. This can seem frustrating, but remember your end goal: Increase your overall test scores to a level where you're consistently scoring 80 percent or higher. It usually takes one month to raise your average test score 5 percent. To achieve this, you'll need to get into the habit of finding out why you missed each question that you did. Then commit the facts of the question to memory so you won't miss a similar question in the future.

The 225-question Diagnostic Practice Exam included in this guide will serve as your benchmark, and help you determine how much work is ahead of you. For example, if you score 65 percent on the Diagnostic Practice Exam, you'll need to study an additional three months before you're prepared for the exam. (Because it takes one month to raise your average test score 5 percent, it will take three months to increase your score 15 percent.)

The Diagnostic Practice Exam also serves as your study guide. For each question you attempt, read the answer that follows and make sure you understand the key details of the question. If you find a topic that is particularly difficult for you, make a note of it, and do additional research. The biggest obstacle to passing the exam is recognizing your problem areas so you can focus your time and energy accordingly. By using the Diagnostic Practice Exam as your roadmap, you'll quickly and easily be able to pinpoint the areas where you need to spend additional time studying. Once you've mastered each topic, retake the exam to check your progress.

TRACKING YOUR PROGRESS

Use the blank worksheets provided in the Appendix to track your progress. You should become familiar with two worksheets.

1. Study Journal

On the *Study Journal*, record the date you studied, the length of time you studied, and the source of your study materials. Also list the subjects you focused your attention on (e.g., Investments, Retirement Planning, Estate Planning, etc.). Record any milestones you surpassed, such as "reached one hundred hours of study time", or "finished reading Keir book for the second time". You goal is to study at least three hundred hours by test day. A blank *Study Journal* and a partially completed sample are provided in the Appendix.

2. Practice Test Results

On the worksheet labeled *Practice Test Results*, record the number of times you worked on a particular set of questions, the source of the questions, how many questions you answered correctly, and how many you attempted. Then add up your figures at the bottom of the page. You should attempt at least five thousand questions prior to taking the exam, and your scores should exceed 80 percent by test day. A blank *Practice Test Results* worksheet and a partially completed sample are provided in the Appendix.

RECOMMENDED STUDY SCHEDULE

The following study schedule should be repeated each week until the exam. If you follow the schedule, you'll achieve eighteen hours of studying per week, and three hundred hours in just over four months. It's important not to skip a day and to maintain a consistent pace. Of course, life gets in the way and it may not be possible to follow the prescribed schedule each day. If you're forced to miss a day, try to make it up as soon as possible. If you find yourself consistently falling behind, you should consider taking the exam at a later date.

Day 1	Sunday	1 hour organizing notes and developing study plan 3 hours of case questions	4 hours
Day 2	Monday	2 hours of multiple choice questions	2 hours
Day 3	Tuesday	2 hours of multiple choice questions	2 hours
Day 4	Wednesday	2 hours studying notes only Take a break from multiple choice questions	2 hours
Day 5	Thursday	2 hours of case questions	2 hours
Day 6	Friday	2 hours of multiple choice questions	2 hours
Day 7	Saturday	4 hours of multiple choice questions Focus on your weakest subjects from the past week	4 hours
			18 hours

You need to study the day before, and the day of, the exam. Some CFP® review providers say it's best to "clear your head" before the exam. I disagree. You need to use the hours leading up to the exam to absorb any last minute details. As a first-time exam passer (passed March 2008), I can personally tell you it's amazing how much knowledge you'll lose once the test is over, and just how quickly it will go. With that in mind, you need to make studying stress free within twenty-four hours of the exam, and use that time effectively as a refresher. Part 2 of this guide provides six unit summaries with key facts you need to know for the exam. You should study the six unit summaries during the twenty-four hour period leading up to the exam.

EXAM FORMAT

The CFP® Certification Exam is a ten-hour exam divided into two days.

- Four-hour session on Friday afternoon: 115 questions, including a long case
- Three-hour session on Saturday morning: 85 questions, including a long case
- Three-hour session on Saturday afternoon: 85 questions, including a long case

I recommend completing the long case last in each session (case strategy will be discussed in Part 4 of this guide). There are 285 questions on the exam, and approximately 225 questions will be unrelated to the cases. For this reason, the Diagnostic Practice Exam includes 225 questions.

Of the three sessions you'll face, one will always seem more difficult than the others. Anticipate this and move on. I have not heard of a CFP® exam where all three sessions were equally as difficult in the eyes of the test takers. Don't be discouraged if your Friday session is difficult, it will get easier.

Based on the "Topic List For CFP® Certification Examination" provided by the CFP® Board, the estimated breakdown for the exam is:

• Investment Planning	19%	54 questions
• Retirement Planning	19%	54 questions
• Estate Planning	15%	43 questions
• Insurance and Risk	14%	40 questions
• Income Tax Planning	14%	40 questions
• General Principles	11%	31 questions
• Employee Benefits	8%	23 questions
	100%	285 questions

You should allocate your study time according to these percentages, as well. Don't fall into the trap of ignoring the General Principles section. These questions account for 11 percent of the total exam, and may mean the difference between passing and failing.

Exam questions are presented in two multiple choice formats:

1. Basic-type multiple choice question: A, B, C, D are given, and you must select the single best answer.

2. Combination-type multiple choice question: (1), (2), (3), (4) are given, and one, some, all, or none of the choices may be correct. You must select the correct combination of choices.

Matching-type questions are being phased out of the exam, but remain one of the best ways to test your knowledge. For this reason, matching-type questions are included in the Diagnostic Practice Exam.

EXAM PROVIDED MATERIALS

When you take the CFP® Certification Exam you'll be provided with the following information:

- Tax tables for individuals, corporations, estates, and trusts
- Standard deduction amounts
- Phaseouts for itemized deductions and personal exemptions
- Estate and gift tax tables
- Applicable credit amounts

You'll also receive the following formula sheet:

$$V = \frac{D_1}{r-g}$$

$$r_i = r_f + (r_m - r_f)\beta_i$$

$$r = \frac{D_1}{P} + g$$

$$r_p = r_f + \sigma_p \left(\frac{r_m - r_f}{\sigma_m} \right)$$

$$COV_{ij} = \rho_{ij}\sigma_i\sigma_j$$

$$S_p = \frac{\overline{r_p} - \overline{r_f}}{\sigma_p}$$

$$\sigma_p = \sqrt{W_i^2\sigma_i^2 + W_j^2\sigma_j^2 + 2W_iW_jCOV_{ij}}$$

$$\alpha_p = \overline{r_p} - \left[\overline{r_f} + \left(\overline{r_m} - \overline{r_f} \right)\beta_p \right]$$

$$\beta_i = \frac{COV_{im}}{\sigma_m^2} = \frac{\rho_{im}\sigma_i}{\sigma_m}$$

$$T_p = \frac{\overline{r_p} - \overline{r_f}}{\beta_p}$$

$$\sigma_r = \sqrt{\frac{\sum_{t=1}^{n}(r_t - \overline{r})^2}{n}}$$

$$D = \frac{\sum_{t=1}^{n}\frac{c_t(t)}{(1+i)^t}}{\sum_{t=1}^{n}\frac{c_t}{(1+i)^t}}$$

$$S_r = \sqrt{\frac{\sum_{t=1}^{n}(r_t - \overline{r})^2}{n-1}}$$

$$D = \frac{1+y}{y} - \frac{(1+y)+t(c-y)}{c\left[(1+y)^t - 1\right]+y}$$

$$CV = \frac{Par}{CP} \times P_s$$

$$\frac{\Delta P}{P} = -D\left[\frac{\Delta y}{1+y}\right]$$

$$IR = \frac{R_P - R_B}{\sigma_A}$$

To make studying more productive, commit the following *labeled* formula sheet to memory. Then read the summary that follows, and make sure you understand the meaning of the variables. But keep in mind, the formula sheet you receive on the exam will not be labeled.

1. Value: Constant Dividend Growth Model

$$V = \frac{D_1}{r - g}$$

2. Return: Constant Dividend Growth Model

$$r = \frac{D_1}{P} + g$$

3. Covariance

$$COV_{ij} = \rho_{ij}\sigma_i\sigma_j$$

4. Standard Deviation of a Portfolio

$$\sigma_p = \sqrt{W_i^2\sigma_i^2 + W_j^2\sigma_j^2 + 2W_iW_j COV_{ij}}$$

5. Beta

$$\beta_i = \frac{COV_{im}}{\sigma_m^2} = \frac{\rho_{im}\sigma_i}{\sigma_m}$$

6. Population Standard Deviation

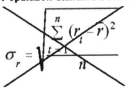

$$\sigma_r = \sqrt{\frac{\sum_{t=1}^{n}(r_i - r)^2}{n}}$$

7. Sample Standard Deviation

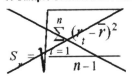

$$S = \sqrt{\frac{\sum_{t=1}^{n}(r_t - r)^2}{n-1}}$$

8. Conversion Value of a Bond

$$CV = \frac{Par}{CP} \times P_s$$

9. CAPM

$$r_i = r_f + (r_m - r_f)\beta_i$$

10. Required Return: Security Market Line

$$r_p = r_f + \sigma_p\left(\frac{r_m - r_f}{\sigma_m}\right)$$

11. Sharpe

$$S_p = \frac{\overline{r}_p - \overline{r}_f}{\sigma_p}$$

12. Jensen's Alpha

$$\alpha_p = \overline{r}_p - \left[\overline{r}_f + \left(\overline{r}_m - \overline{r}_f\right)\beta_p\right]$$

13. Treynor

$$T_p = \frac{\overline{r}_p - \overline{r}_f}{\beta_p}$$

14. Duration

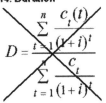

$$D = \frac{\sum_{t=1}^{n}\frac{c_t(t)}{(1+i)^t}}{\sum_{t=1}^{n}\frac{c_t}{(1+i)^t}}$$

15. Duration

$$D = \frac{1+y}{y} - \frac{(1+y) + t(c - y)}{c\left[(1+y)^t - 1\right] + y}$$

16. Percentage Change in Bond Price

$$\frac{\Delta P}{P} = -D\left[\frac{\Delta y}{1+y}\right]$$

17. Information Ratio

$$IR = \frac{R_P - R_B}{\sigma_A}$$

Formula Sheet Summary

- You will never use formulas 6, 7, and 14
- You will rarely use formulas 8, 16, and 17
- Formulas 1 and 2 are similar
- In formulas 1 and 2: $D_1 = D_0 (1+g)$
- Formula 9 can be found inside formula 12

The variables listed within the formulas are defined as follows:

cov = covariance	ΔP = change in bond price	V = value
CV = conversion value	r = return	W = weight
D_0 = dividend today	r_m = return of the market	y = yield to maturity
D_1 = dividend in one year	r_p = return of the portfolio	Δy = change in interest rates
D = duration	r_f = risk-free rate	a = alpha (Jensen's alpha)
g = growth rate of dividends	r = average return	ß = beta
IR = information ratio	S = Sharpe	p = correlation coefficient
P = price	t = time	o = standard deviation
Par = par price of bond	T = Treynor	c = coupon

You should reach the point where any time you see a calculation question, you're confident you'll get it correct. You should welcome calculation questions because they're less subjective and often based on a formula. Your biggest enemy on the exam will be the ambiguous questions that could have multiple right answers. If you're not proficient with your calculator or the formula sheet, do additional practice problems until you're scoring 80 percent or better.

TEST TAKING STRATEGY

There is a simple test taking strategy you can follow that will alleviate stress and put you in the best possible position to pass the exam. Use the following strategy for each session of the exam:

Step 1:   Go through the exam one time and try to answer each question. If you can't determine an answer, circle the question and move on. Having ten to twenty circled questions your first time through each session is reasonable.

Step 2:   Once you've made your first pass through the exam, go back and answer the questions you circled. Hopefully you found a few additional answers by finishing the exam and *using the exam to your advantage.*

Step 3:   If you still can't settle on an answer, highlight the question so you know you need to come back to it yet again. You should have to highlight no more than four or five questions.

Step 4:   Go back over the exam a final time and answer the highlighted questions. Even if you need to guess, mark down an answer so you have a chance of getting it correct. If you only have four or five questions you're "guessing" on, you're doing great.

Time should not be a factor on the exam. If you follow the strategy provided, and you're scoring 80 percent or higher on practice tests, then you should finish each session with about thirty minutes to spare. This means the ten-hour exam is reduced to only eight and a half hours of concentration. Spread over two days, with a break on the second day, it's not as strenuous as you may have thought. It will be easier than you think to stay fresh for that long.

Additional Thoughts

I've heard it said there are ten thousand possible questions for the exam and 285 are chosen at random. While I doubt this is accurate, I do believe it's true that roughly 3 percent of everything you learned will be tested. This means you need to learn it all, but don't be surprised if particular topics you studied are left out entirely.

It's important to learn from the experiences of others. There's a helpful discussion forum available for free at www.financial-planning.com. On this website, there is a Career Development section where participants are invited to discuss how they prepared for the CFP® Certification Exam. By participating in these online discussions, you'll learn best practices and reinforce positive study habits.

SUMMARY OF HOW TO USE THIS GUIDE

Step 1:   Take the Diagnostic Practice Exam to see where you stand today and identify your weak areas. Scoring between 50 percent and 70 percent your first time through is average.

Step 2:   Follow the recommended study schedule to raise your test scores to 80 percent or higher. Generally, an increase of 5 percent per month can be achieved if you follow the provided study schedule.

Step 3: Determine the date you'd like to take the exam based on the 5 percent per month rule. For example, if you're currently scoring 60 percent on practice tests, you'll need to study an additional four months to reach 80 percent.

Step 4: Use the blank worksheets provided in the Appendix to carefully track your progress.

Step 5: Reach a plateau by test day. If you continue scoring higher in the days immediately leading up to the exam, you may need additional study time. By the time you reach the exam, you should be reinforcing topics already learned, rather than learning new ones. Most test takers who successfully complete the exam reach a plateau between 80 percent and 85 percent by test day.

Part 2:

UNIT SUMMARIES

GENERAL PRINCIPLES OF FINANCIAL PLANNING

1. Code of Ethics
- Two Parts: Part 1 – Principles, Part 2 – Rules
- There are seven principles and you need to know them in order
  The seven principles form the acronym "IOCFCPD"
  Ideas Only Come From Careful Planning Daily
- There are two "C's" (competence and confidentiality) and you need to know where each is located among the principles

Principle 1: Integrity
- No false or misleading advertising
- No dishonesty, fraud, or deceit
- Don't commingle client funds
- Show the care of a fiduciary

Principle 2: Objectivity
- Use reasonable and prudent professional judgment
- Act in the interest of the client

Principle 3: Competency
- Complete continuing education requirements
- Only advise clients in areas where you're competent

Principle 4: Fairness
- Disclose conflicts of interest
- Disclose your firm's basic information
- Disclose compensation sources
- Provide ADV to client
- Client's fee must be fair and reasonable
- Provide timely information about any change of employment

Principle 5: Confidentiality
- Show the same confidentiality to employers and clients

Principle 6: Professionalism
- Use of CFP® marks
- Tell CFP® Board if advisor violates code
- Can't write RIA – must use Registered Investment Advisor
- Return client records in a timely manner

Principle 7: Diligence
- Only work with clients if it's warranted based on their needs and objectives
- Make and/or implement only suitable recommendations

2. Financial Planning Steps
- Establish
- Gather
- Analyze
- Develop
- Implement
- Monitor

3. Debt Ratios
- Housing costs ≤ 28% of gross income
- Consumer debt ≤ 20% of net income
- Total debt ≤ 36% of gross income

4. Fiscal vs. Monetary Policy
- Fiscal policy: taxes, public spending, and government borrowing
- Monetary policy: required reserve ratio, open market operations, and discount rate

5. Expansionary vs. Contractionary Policy
- Expansionary policy: taxes go down, public spending goes up, and government borrowing goes up
- Contractionary policy: taxes go up, public spending goes down, and government borrowing goes down

INSURANCE PLANNING AND RISK MANAGEMENT

1. Homeowners Insurance Covered Perils

Form	Type	Dwelling	Personal Property
HO-2	Home	Broad	Broad
HO-3	Home	Open	Broad
HO-5	Home	Open	Open
HO-4	Renters	None	Broad
HO-6	Condo	None	Broad
HO-8	Old Home	Replacement cost in excess of market value	

2. Amount paid by insurance company for homeowners claim
- [(insurance carried / insurance required) x loss] − deductible = amount paid by insurance company

3. Covered Perils
a. Basic Form: HARVEST WFL
- Hail, Aircraft, Riot, Vandalism, Vehicles, Volcanic eruption, Explosion, Smoke, Theft, Windstorm, Fire, Lightning

b. Broad Form: Basic Form + FAR
- Falling objects, Freezing pipes, Artificially generated electricity, Ruptured system

c. Open Form: All-Risk Coverage
- Policy lists perils not covered, and the loss from any peril not excluded is covered

4. Life Insurance Non-Forfeiture Options
- Cash
- Extended-term
- Paid-up reduced amount

5. Life Insurance Dividend Options
- Cash
- Paid-up additions
- Accumulate with interest
- Premium reduction
- One-year term (5th dividend)

6. Life Insurance Settlement Options
- Cash
- Refund option
- Period certain and life
- Pure life or single life
- Specified period
- Specified income

7. Stop Loss vs. Stop Loss Limit
- Stop loss: Maximum out-of-pocket cost the insured will have to pay (better for the insurer)
- Stop loss limit: Amount of expenses after the deductible that are split between the insurer and the insured (better for the insured)

8. Annuity Date
- 8/13/82
- Annuity contracts issued after 8/13/82 are taxed as LIFO (last in, first out), with interest taxed first.

9. MEC Date
- 6/21/88
- Single premium life insurance policies issued after 6/21/88 are treated as modified endowment contracts (MECs). Distributions are taxed as LIFO (last in, first out), with interest taxed first.
- You need to memorize the dates for annuities and MECs.

INCOME TAX PLANNING

1. Tax Penalties
- Failure to pay: 0.5% of the tax due per month, up to a maximum of 25%
- Failure to file: 5% of the tax due per month, up to a maximum of 25%
- Negligence: 20% of the underpayment attributed to negligence
- Civil fraud: 75% of the underpayment attributed to civil fraud
- Tax return preparer understates the amount of tax owed: $1,000 penalty
- Don't confuse the failure to file penalty with the failure to pay penalty.

2. Personal Service Corporation (PSC)
- Any income retained by a PSC is taxed at a flat 35% rate instead of the graduated corporate tax rates.
- A closely held C Corp is a PSC if it falls into one of the categories of the acronym "HEAL".
- Health (doctors, dentists, etc.)
  Engineering
  Accounting, Architectural
  Law

3. Depreciation Property Classes
- 5 year property   1245 property   Autos, light duty trucks, computers
- 7 year property   1245 property   Office equipment except computers
- 27½ year property   1250 property   Residential realty
- 39 year property   1250 property   Commercial realty

4. AMT Preference Items and Adjustments
- Remember the acronym "IPOD".
- Incentive stock option bargain element
  Private activity municipal bonds
  Oil and gas percentage depletion
  Depreciation (ACRS and MACRS)

5. Charitable Contributions

	Public Organization	Private Organization
Ordinary Income Property (STCG, use-unrelated tangible personalty, cash, self-constructed)	50%	30%
Fair Market Value Property (LTCG, use-related tangible personalty)	30%	20%

6. Self-Employment Tax

- To calculate the self-employment tax, multiply the total self-employment income by 14.13%. To find the allowable one-half self-employment tax deduction, divide your answer by two.

7. Estimated Tax Payments

- The required annual payment is the lesser of 90% of the current year's estimated tax bill, or 100% of last year's tax bill. If last year's tax return showed income over $150,000, you must pay 110% instead of 100%.

8. Casualty and Theft Losses

- Step 1: Start with the lesser of the property's basis or FMV
- Step 2: Subtract insurance coverage
- Step 3: Subtract $100 floor
- Step 4: Subtract 10% of AGI
- Step 5: The result is the deductible casualty loss

INVESTMENT PLANNING

1. ISOs vs. NSOs

- Incentive stock options (ISOs) must be held for at least one year from the date of exercise and two years from the date of grant before selling them. Otherwise, they become nonqualified stock options (NSOs).
- Example: What are the taxes owed on 1,000 shares of stock with an exercise price of $10 per share?

	ISO	NSO
Employee exercises when the FMV is $20 per share	No tax is paid (AMT preference item)	($20 - $10) x 1,000 shares = $10,000 $10,000 x ordinary income tax = tax paid
Employee sells stock at $30 per share after holding for more than one year	($30 - $10) x 1,000 shares = $20,000 $20,000 x capital gains rate = tax paid	($30 - $20) x 1,000 shares = $10,000 $10,000 x capital gains rate = tax paid

2. Bond Relationships

- The smaller the bond's coupon, the greater the relative price fluctuation
- The smaller the bond's coupon, the lower the reinvestment rate risk
- The lower the interest rate, the greater the relative price fluctuation
- The longer the term to maturity, the greater the relative price fluctuation
- Higher inflation = higher interest rates = lower bond values

3. Duration Relationships

- Higher coupon = lower duration = lower interest rate risk
- As interest rates decrease, duration increases
- As interest rates increase, duration decreases

4. Beta vs. Standard Deviation

- Beta and standard deviation are used to compare securities
- If R^2 is high (>0.60), then beta is the relevant measure to use when comparing securities. The beta measures are Jensen's alpha and Treynor.
- If R^2 is low (<0.60), then standard deviation is the relevant measure to use when comparing securities. The standard deviation measure is Sharpe.
- R^2 is the Coefficient of Determination and measures systematic risk.
- ($1 - R^2$ = unsystematic risk)

5. Puts and Calls
- A put gives the holder the right to sell a security. Remember the acronym "PS" for "Put = Sell".
- A call gives the holder the right to buy a security. Remember the acronym "BC" for "Buy Calls".
- Buying a call and selling a put are both bullish strategies.
- Buying a put and selling a call are both bearish strategies.
- An investor who expects a large price fluctuation, either up or down, should buy a call or put, respectively.
- An investor who expects a small price fluctuation, either up or down, should sell a put or call, respectively. An investor sells puts and calls when seeking premium income.
- Straddle: Buying a put and buying a call
- Collar: Buying a put and selling a call
- Selling = writing = taking the short position

6. Legislation
- Securities Act of 1933: Regulates new securities
- Securities Act of 1934: Regulates existing securities
- Investment Company Act of 1940: Regulates mutual funds
- SIPC of 1970: Regulates brokerage firms

7. Margin Call
- [(1 − initial margin percentage) / (1 − maintenance margin percentage)] x purchase price of the stock = margin call

8. Taxable Equivalent Yield
- [(tax exempt yield) / (1 − marginal tax rate)] = taxable equivalent yield

RETIREMENT PLANNING

1. 2010 IRA Deduction Phaseouts
- $56,000 - $66,000 if single and active participant
- $89,000 - $109,000 if MFJ and active participant
- $10,000 if married filing separately and active participant
- $167,000 - $177,000 for spouse of active participant and MFJ

2. 2010 Roth IRA Phaseouts
- $105,000 - $120,000 if single
- $166,000 - $176,000 if MFJ

3. 2010 Key Employee
- >5% owner
- Officer with compensation >$160,000
- 1% owner with compensation >$150,000

4. Top Heavy Plans
- A plan is top heavy if >60% of the benefits are attributed to key employees.
- If top heavy, then the minimum contribution the employer must make on behalf of non-key employees is 2% for defined benefit (DB) plans and 3% for defined contribution (DC) plans.
- DB plan: B = second letter of alphabet = 2% contribution
- DC plan: C = third letter of alphabet = 3% contribution

5. Maximum Retirement Plan Contribution for Owner/Employee
- 25% contribution plan = 18.59% x net income
- 15% contribution plan = 12.12% x net income

6. 401k Loans and Withdrawals
- The maximum loan from a 401k is the lesser of $50,000 or one-half the accrued benefit. Accrued benefits include earnings, forfeitures, and employer contributions.
- A hardship withdrawal from a 401k is available for employee contributions only.

7. 2010 Social Security Taxation
- Single: $25,000 to $34,000 = 50% taxable
  $34,001 or greater = 85% taxable
- MFJ: $32,000 to $44,000 = 50% taxable
  $44,001 or greater = 85% taxable

8. Retirement Needs Calculation

- **Step 1: Calculate the future value of the income needed**
  End mode
  PV = value provided in today's dollars
  i = inflation
  n = number of years until retirement
  Solve for FV

- **Step 2: Calculate the present value of the serial payments**
  Begin mode
  FV from Step 1 becomes PMT for Step 2
  i = inflation adjusted return: [(1 + return / 1 + inflation rate) − 1]
  n = number of years from retirement until death
  Solve for PV

- **Step 3: Total amount needed**
  End mode
  PV from Step 2 becomes FV for Step 3
  i = investment return
  n = number of years until retirement
  Solve for PV

ESTATE PLANNING

1. Probate
- JTWROS (spouse): Avoids probate
- JTWROS (non-spouse): Avoids probate
- Tenancy by entirety: Avoids probate
- Tenancy in common: Goes to probate
- Community property: Goes to probate

2. Included in Gross Estate
- JTWROS (spouse): Half the property is included in the gross estate of the decedent regardless of contribution
- JTWROS (non-spouse): Full value of the property is included in the gross estate of the decedent unless the survivor shows consideration furnished
- Tenancy by entirety: Half the property is included in the gross estate of the decedent regardless of contribution
- Tenancy in common: Fractional ownership of the property is included in the gross estate
- Community property: Half the property is included in the gross estate of the decedent regardless of contribution

3. Step-Up in Basis
- JTWROS (spouse): Step-up in basis for the one-half property
- JTWROS (non-spouse): Full step-up in basis to the extent the property is included in the decedent's gross estate
- Tenancy by entirety: Step-up in basis for the one-half property
- Tenancy in common: Full step-up in basis
- Community property: Step-up in basis for entire property

4. Miscellaneous Property Ownership Rules
- Tenancy by entirety is only allowed for spouses. Property is protected from the claims of each spouse's separate creditors, but not from the claims of both spouses' joint creditors.
- Community property states allow each spouse to transfer his/her half interest at death as he/she wants, but not during life without the consent of the spouse.

5. GSTT Tax
- Direct Skip: Transferor pays tax
- Taxable Termination: Trustee pays tax
- Taxable Distribution: Transferee pays tax

6. Estate Tax Calculation

- **Gross Estate**
  - subtract debts, funeral expenses, administrative expenses
  - subtract casualty and theft losses
  - subtract state death tax
  - **Adjusted Gross Estate**
  - subtract marital deduction
  - subtract charitable deduction
  - **Taxable Estate**
  - + add adjusted taxable gifts
  - **Tentative Tax Base**
  - x multiply by the estate tax rate
  - **Tentative Tax**
  - subtract gift taxes paid on post-1976 gifts
  - subtract credit for taxes paid on pre-1977 gifts
  - subtract unified credit
  - subtract foreign death tax credit
  - subtract credit for tax on prior transfers
  - **Net Estate Tax**
  - + add GSTT
  - **Total Estate Tax**

7. Estate Tax Information

	2009	2010
Estate tax exemption	$3,500,000	Tax Repeal
Applicable credit	$1,455,800	Tax Repeal
GSTT exemption	$3,500,000	Tax Repeal
Gift tax exemption	$1,000,000	$1,000,000
Annual gift exclusion	$13,000	$13,000

Part 3:

DIAGNOSTIC PRACTICE EXAM

QUESTIONS

1. Your client is starting a new business and his highest priority is limiting his personal liability. In addition, he would like to have flow-through taxation, and the ability to sell interests in his business easily in the future. Which of the following entities is most appropriate to meet your client's goals?

   A. Sole proprietorship
   B. Limited partnership
   C. S Corp
   D. C Corp

2. Which of the following is correct regarding IRA contributions?

   A. IRA contributions made above the maximum annual limit are subject to a 10% nondeductible excise tax.
   B. A nonworking divorced person, over the age of 50, who receives alimony may contribute to an IRA the lesser of $6,000 or 100% of the alimony received.
   C. An employee who makes voluntary contributions to a retirement plan is not considered an active participant.
   D. An employee participating in a 457 plan is considered an active participant.

3. Which of the following are included as part of the third step of the financial planning process?

   (1) Identifying the client's financial strengths and weaknesses
   (2) Considering options available for the achievement of goals
   (3) Developing a schedule for implementation
   (4) Selecting appropriate strategies for the achievement of goals

   A. (1) only
   B. (4) only
   C. (1) and (2) only
   D. (3) and (4) only

4. Your client asks you to explain how itemized deductions will impact her taxes. You tell her that itemized deductions are:

   A. Trade or business expenses deductible in arriving at gross income
   B. Personal expenses deductible in arriving at gross income
   C. Trade or business expenses deductible from AGI
   D. Personal expenses deductible from AGI

5. Tyler received a tip from his friend about a new mutual fund he should consider adding to his portfolio. He wanted to determine if the fund was appropriate, so he searched the Internet and found the following data: standard deviation is high, R^2 is 0.30, alpha is high, and the beta is 0.70. What should you tell Tyler about the data he collected?

A. Beta is significant
B. Alpha is significant
C. The Jensen calculation is significant
D. The Sharpe calculation is significant

6. Your client is concerned about maintaining her privacy and wants to avoid probate at death. Which of her assets would be subject to probate?

(1) A condo she owns in common with her husband
(2) An annuity that names her husband as beneficiary
(3) Land owned jointly (JTWROS) with her daughter that your client contributed all the money to purchase
(4) Her sole proprietorship dog-grooming business
(5) A $500,000 life insurance policy payable to her estate

A. (3) and (4) only
B. (1), (3), and (5) only
C. (1), (4), and (5) only
D. All of the above

For questions 7-9, match the disability policy renewal provision with the description that follows. Use only one answer per blank. Answers may be used more than once or not at all.

A. Noncancellable
B. Cancelable
C. Conditionally renewable
D. Guaranteed renewable

7. _____ The insurer has the right not to renew the policy for specific reasons listed in the contract.

8. _____ The premium schedule will never change unless the insured buys more coverage in the future.

9. _____ The insurer cannot change the premium unless the change is made for an entire class of policyholders.

10. **Dr. Bowman, age 29, recently opened a successful dental practice. He's concerned that his young employees will leave for a more experienced dental practice once they're fully trained. In order to retain his young employees, which retirement plan should Dr. Bowman adopt?**

    A. Defined benefit plan
    B. Target benefit plan
    C. Money purchase plan
    D. Cash balance plan

11. **Mike had four credit cards in his wallet when it was stolen on the subway. The credit cards were fraudulently used before Mike could report them missing. He provides you with the following amounts that were charged on each card, and asks you to determine his liability. What is Mike's liability for the transactions?**

    Card 1: $650
    Card 2: $50
    Card 3: $375
    Card 4: $25

    A. $50
    B. $175
    C. $200
    D. $1,100

12. **Which of the following is a requirement for a business to make a valid S Corp election?**

    A. A simple majority of shareholders must consent to the election.
    B. All shareholders must be US citizens, or residents, or a qualifying trust.
    C. There may be no more than 75 employees.
    D. There may be no more than two classes of stock.

13. **The rate of return calculated by the capital asset pricing model (CAPM) is:**

    A. The rate of return used to represent the market's overall rate of return
    B. Not reliable because CAPM uses standard deviation in its formula
    C. The rate of return used in the dividend growth model for valuing common stock
    D. Not reliable because CAPM fails to take risk into account

14. **Peggy recently adopted a profit sharing plan for her pharmacy, but she's unsure about the contribution rules. She'd like to know if she, as the employer, can contribute more than 25% to an employee's account. Which of the following should you tell her?**

    A. Yes, the limit is the lesser of 100% or $49,000
    B. No, the limit is 25%
    C. Yes, but the total company contributions cannot exceed 25% of total plan compensation
    D. Both A and C are correct

For questions 15-21, match the following assets with their appropriate treatment at death. Use only one answer per blank. Answers may be used more than once or not at all.

    A. Included in gross estate / Goes through probate
    B. Included in gross estate / Avoids probate
    C. Excluded from gross estate / Avoids probate
    D. No effect

15. ____ **Payable on death account**

16. ____ **IRA without a named beneficiary**

17. ____ **Apartment building held as tenancy in common**

18. ____ **Restaurant owned by the decedent**

19. ____ **Bank account held as tenancy by entirety**

20. ____ **Testamentary trust**

21. ____ **Home held as community property**

22. **Which of the following is a basic provision of long-term care insurance?**

    A. Premiums paid are deductible in full each year
    B. Premiums are never deductible
    C. Premiums paid are included as deductible medical expenses subject to the 10% of AGI floor
    D. Unreimbursed expenses are subject to the 7½% of AGI floor

23. **Dr. Singh heard from a colleague that he should buy ETFs instead of index mutual funds for his portfolio. He'd like to know if this is good advice, and asks you to explain the advantages ETFs hold over mutual funds. You tell him which of the following?**

(1) Unlike mutual funds, investors can buy and sell ETFs any time during the trading day.
(2) ETFs can be bought on margin or sold short.
(3) There is no transaction fee to buy or sell an ETF.
(4) ETFs have low management fees compared to mutual funds.

A. (3) only
B. (4) only
C. (1), (2), and (3) only
D. (1), (2), and (4) only

24. **Which of the following are tax-free employee benefits a dentist can provide to her employees?**

(1) $60 per month for parking
(2) Occasional sporting event tickets
(3) 50% off dental work
(4) Group disability benefits up to 50% of salary

A. (2) and (3) only
B. (3) and (4) only
C. (1), (2), and (4) only
D. All of the above

25. **All of the following are characteristics of defined contribution plans, except:**

A. The risk of pre-retirement inflation falls on the employer.
B. There are defined employer contributions.
C. The employee assumes the risk of investment performance.
D. Benefits cannot be provided for past service.

26. **Mr. and Mrs. Simpson have lived in a community property state all their married lives. They own a four-story house, registered only in Mrs. Simpson's name. If Mrs. Simpson dies, what will happen to the house?**

    A. The house will pass to Mrs. Simpson's next of kin.
    B. Mrs. Simpson's half will pass by will. Mr. Simpson already owns half under community property laws.
    C. The house will pass to Mr. Simpson.
    D. The house will pass through Mrs. Simpson's will, and the entire house will go to Mr. Simpson.

27. **Stephen, age 28, has a wife and two children. He earns a high income but manages to save very little. Unfortunately, Stephen doesn't think this will ever change. He'd like to purchase a life insurance policy that will force him to save money. Which insurance policy is most suitable to meet Stephen's goals?**

    A. Second-to-die whole life
    B. 20-year term
    C. Universal life
    D. Whole life

28. **Which of the following option strategies is profitable in a rising stock market?**

    (1) Buying a call
    (2) Selling a call
    (3) Buying a put
    (4) Selling a put

    A. (1) and (3) only
    B. (1) and (4) only
    C. (2) and (3) only
    D. (2) and (4) only

29. Terry (AGI of $120,000) has an investment interest expense of $11,000 from her margin account, and has $9,000 of investment income. She paid her investment advisor $4,000 for investment advice this year. How much investment interest expense can Terry deduct?

    A. $4,000
    B. $7,400
    C. $9,400
    D. $11,000

30. Which of the following accurately describes a complex trust?

    A. A trust with more than one beneficiary
    B. A trust that may distribute income annually
    C. A trust that reverts back to the grantor's estate at death
    D. A trust that is required to distribute all of its income annually

31. Which of the following is true regarding profit sharing plan allocation formulas?

    A. Allocation formulas may discriminate in favor of highly compensated employees without penalty.
    B. Contributions may not be skewed to favor older employees.
    C. Allocation formulas must be definite and predetermined.
    D. Employee contributions must be allocated on a pro-rata basis.

32. Dennis wants to set up an irrevocable trust for his less fortunate brother, Paul. Dennis plans to gift $350,000 to the trust and attach Crummey powers. If Paul chooses to exercise his demand right, how much can he withdraw during the first thirty days?

    A. $0
    B. $5,000
    C. $13,000
    D. $17,500

33. **Which entity imposes the reporting and disclosure requirements for defined benefit plans?**

    A. SEC
    B. IRS
    C. ERISA
    D. PBGC

34. **Michelle takes out a $150,000, 15-year fixed mortgage at 6.50%. How much interest will she pay by the end of the loan period?**

    A. $85,199
    B. $113,299
    C. $150,000
    D. $161,415

35. **Mark, age 62, is in poor health. He's currently covered by his large company's health insurance plan, but he isn't sure how much longer he'll be healthy enough to work. How long does Mark need to work to ensure he maintains his health coverage? (Assume Mark will not qualify for health insurance through a private insurer.)**

    A. Until age 63½
    B. Until age 65
    C. Until death
    D. Mark can retire today.

36. **Which of the following is a characteristic of American Depository Receipts (ADRs)?**

    A. ADRs trade once per day like mutual funds.
    B. ADR dividends are declared in US dollars.
    C. ADRs allow domestic securities to be traded in foreign countries.
    D. ADR holders receive foreign tax credits for income tax paid to a foreign country.

37. The S&P index has _____ risk.

A. non-systematic
B. non-diversifiable
C. diversifiable
D. unsystematic

38. Dr. Lyons lives in Ohio but owns real estate in Colorado. He'd like to avoid the cost and delays of ancillary probate. Which of the following are suitable methods for Dr. Lyons to achieve his goal?

(1) Revocable living trust
(2) Irrevocable trust
(3) Deed delivered to an escrow agent
(4) JTWROS
(5) Testamentary trust

A. (2) and (3) only
B. (1), (3), and (4) only
C. (1), (2), (3), and (4) only
D. All of the above

39. Susan owns a beach house in South Carolina that she rents out five months of the year. How many days can she personally use the condo without losing federal income tax deductions?

A. 0 days
B. 7 days
C. 14 days
D. 15 days

40. Mary, a self-employed insurance agent, is concerned that she has not made enough estimated tax payments this year. She wants to avoid the underpayment penalty and asks for your advice. She tells you that last year, she had an AGI of $125,000 and paid $27,000 in income taxes. She expects her tax liability this year to be $24,000. What is the minimum estimated tax payment Mary must make in order to avoid the underpayment penalty?

A. $21,600
B. $24,000
C. $27,000
D. $39,700

41. Which of the following entities are subject to graduated corporate income tax rates?

(1) S Corp
(2) C Corp
(3) LLC
(4) Personal Service Corporation (PSC)

A. (2) only
B. (1) and (3) only
C. (2) and (4) only
D. All of the above

42. Which of the following compensation plans will most likely be subject to forfeiture for the misconduct or termination of an executive?

A. ISO
B. NSO
C. Restricted stock
D. SAR

43. A stock with a beta of -1.5 and a standard deviation of 10.1 will change in which of the following ways if the stock market increases 8%?

A. Increase by 4%
B. Increase by 8%
C. Decrease by 10.1%
D. Decrease by 12%

44. Based on the Markowitz model, which of the following securities would a rational investor choose?

A. Rate of return 7%, beta 1.2
B. Rate of return 9%, beta 1.1
C. Rate of return 10%, beta 1.0
D. Rate of return 10%, beta 1.1

45. **Your client, a wealthy widow, is considering a prenuptial agreement before beginning her second marriage. You inform her that a prenuptial agreement is intended to address which of the following issues?**

A. Who will be responsible for child support payments
B. Who will pay alimony to whom, and in what amount
C. Who will gain custody of children born to the marriage
D. Who will own assets brought to the marriage

46. **Jack owns a condo that he would like to pass to his grandchildren at death. Instead of waiting, he gives his grandchildren the condo today with the provision that he can continue to live in it for the rest of his life. Which of the following interests has Jack given?**

A. A remainder interest
B. A reversionary interest
C. A term interest
D. A life estate interest

47. **Which of the following entities will protect owners from liability beyond the amount they personally invested?**

(1) Limited partnership
(2) LLC
(3) Sole proprietorship
(4) C Corp
(5) S Corp

A. (1) and (3) only
B. (2) and (4) only
C. (2), (4), and (5) only
D. All of the above

48. **The standard deviation of an investment portfolio must be _____ the weighted average of the standard deviation of returns of the individual securities.**

A. less than
B. greater than
C. equal to
D. less than or equal to

49. Bret, while starting a bonfire on his property, negligently caused his neighbor's house to catch fire. The neighbor's insurer paid for the damages, and then sued Bret for reimbursement. Which of the following principles gives the insurer this right?

    A. Absolute liability
    B. Attractive nuisance
    C. Subrogation
    D. Estoppel

50. Your client notices that she has separate deductibles on her personal auto policy for "collision" and "other-than-collision" coverage. She asks you to explain the difference. You tell her the following losses would be considered "other-than-collision".

    (1) Flood
    (2) Vandalism
    (3) Falling objects
    (4) Impact with a deer
    (5) Impact with a large tree

    A. (1), (3), and (5) only
    B. (2), (4), and (5) only
    C. (1), (2), (3), and (4) only
    D. (2), (3), (4), and (5) only

51. The duration of a bond is least affected by its _____

    A. time to maturity.
    B. quality.
    C. coupon.
    D. interest rate.

52. Richard has been named the executor of his uncle's estate. Part of his duty as executor is to file the federal estate tax return. On what form is the federal estate tax filed?

    A. Schedule D
    B. Form 706
    C. Form 709
    D. Form 715

53. **Your client wants to make a gift to the United Way and receive an annual guaranteed return of 6% based on the initial gift amount. Which of the following is true regarding this gift and its intended payout?**

    A. A charitable lead trust can accomplish this goal.
    B. A CRAT can accomplish this goal.
    C. A CRUT can accomplish this goal if the trust specifies 6%.
    D. Only a CRAT can accomplish this goal. CRUTs are limited by the "5 by 5" power.

54. **Rita is receiving payments from her ex-husband pursuant to their divorce decree. She asks you to clarify which of her payments are considered alimony. You tell her which of the following will qualify as alimony?**

    A. Paying of child support by Rita's ex-husband
    B. Paying of the payor spouse's mortgage (The payee, Rita, lives in the house.)
    C. Paying $5,000 to Rita's IRA
    D. None of these qualify as alimony.

For questions 55-59, match the type of retirement plan with the description that follows. Use only one answer per blank. Answers may be used more than once or not at all.

    A. Money purchase plan
    B. Target benefit plan
    C. Flat benefit plan
    D. SEP
    E. Cash balance plan
    F. Profit sharing plan
    G. Unit benefit plan

55. ____ **A plan similar to a defined benefit plan because contributions are based on projected retirement benefits**

56. ____ **A type of defined contribution plan that is not a pension plan**

57. ____ **A defined benefit plan that defines the employee's benefit in terms that are more characteristic of a defined contribution plan**

58. ____ **The employer calculates the contribution by multiplying an employee's years of service by a percentage of his or her salary**

59. ____ **A plan that requires a fixed percentage of compensation be contributed for each eligible employee**

For questions 60-64, match the employer-provided fringe benefit with the description that follows. Use only one answer per blank. Answers may be used more than once or not at all.

    A. Includible as taxable income to all employees
    B. Excludible from the taxable income of all employees
    C. Includible as taxable income to highly compensated employees only
    D. Excludible from the taxable income of highly compensated employees only

60. ____ **Air travel for an airline employee**

61. ____ **Membership dues to a business-related association**

62. ____ **Personal use of an employer-provided cottage**

63. ____ **Personal use of a corporate jet**

64. ____ **30% discount on vision services provided by the employer (an optometrist)**

65. **During the recent recession, your client purchased high-yield corporate bonds that now face minimal default risk. However, your client is concerned that the various corporations may decide to call their bonds. You tell him that corporations are likely to call their bonds when _____**

    A. the bonds are selling at a significant premium.
    B. interest rates are expected to drop.
    C. inflation is expected to rise.
    D. interest rates have declined.

66. **COBRA may be provided for 36 months under which of the following circumstances?**

    A. The employee changes from full-time to part-time employment
    B. The employee resigns
    C. The widow and dependents (under age 14) of a covered employee request coverage
    D. The spouse of a covered employee requests coverage after the employee has been terminated

67. Your client is interested in participating in his company's qualified retirement plan. He has completed one year of service and read on the Internet that this makes him eligible to participate. Sadly, his employer won't let him enroll in the plan until next year. You tell your client that eligibility may be postponed until the completion of his second year of service if which of the following apply?

A. The employer agrees to match 100% of employee deferrals up to 10% of compensation.
B. Contributions are made based on an age-weighted formula.
C. Key employees must wait three years to enroll.
D. Contributions are 100% immediately vested upon eligibility.

68. You've been approached by two friends, Bert and Ernie, who would like your advice on a like-kind exchange they're considering. Currently, Bert owns a rental house and Ernie owns a home. Which of the following is true regarding the potential exchange Bert and Ernie are considering?

A. Bert can do a like-kind exchange if he uses the new property for rental purposes.
B. Ernie can do a like-kind exchange if he uses the new property for rental purposes.
C. Both Bert and Ernie are eligible to do a like-kind exchange, as long as the transferred properties are used for rental purposes.
D. Neither Bert nor Ernie are eligible to do a like-kind exchange because Ernie owns a home.

69. Professor Radford inherited low-basis stock that is currently valued at $800,000. In order to maintain his lifestyle, he needs an 8% payout for life. Which of the following techniques would allow Professor Radford to meet his goal?

A. Donor advised fund
B. CRUT
C. CRAT
D. Charitable gift annuity

70. One of your clients is in desperate need of a loan and asks you to personally lend him money. He's willing to pay an above-market interest rate and pledge his assets as collateral. However, you learn that the CFP® Board of Professional Review urges advisors to avoid lending to clients personally. The two most frequently cited rules that apply to this situation are:

   A. Rule 200 (Objectivity) and Rule 600 (Professionalism)
   B. Rule 200 (Fairness) and Rule 300 (Confidentiality)
   C. Rule 500 (Diligence) and Rule 600 (Professionalism)
   D. Rule 400 (Integrity) and Rule 500 (Diligence)

For questions 71-74, match the type of compensation plan with the description that follows. Use only one answer per blank. Answers may be used more than once or not at all.

   A. Excess benefit plan
   B. Supplemental executive retirement plan (SERP)
   C. Unfunded deferred compensation plan
   D. Rabbi trust
   E. Funded deferred compensation plan
   F. Secular trust
   G. Salary reduction plan

71. _____ The plan uses some portion of the employee's current compensation to fund the ultimate benefit.

72. _____ The plan provides a retirement benefit in excess of the company's qualified plan benefit, and without regard to the IRC Section 415 limits.

73. _____ The plan provides the retirement benefit that would be paid under the company's qualified plan formula if the IRC Section 415 limits did not apply.

74. _____ The plan provides the executive only with a promise to pay benefits at retirement.

75. Which of the following are needed for a retiring 58-year-old client who has a good defined benefit plan at her current job?

(1) Long-term care insurance
(2) Life insurance
(3) Disability insurance
(4) Health insurance

A. (1) and (3) only
B. (1) and (4) only
C. (2) and (3) only
D. All of the above

76. Infodyne Worldwide, a growing California IT company, plans to launch its IPO this year. Infodyne's IPO will be regulated by which of the following laws?

A. Securities Act of 1933
B. Securities Act of 1934
C. Investment Company Act of 1940
D. SIPC of 1970

77. Which of the following is true regarding active participation status in retirement plans?

A. An employee participating in a 457 plan is considered an active participant.
B. An employee who makes voluntary contributions to her 403b is not considered an active participant.
C. An employee who does not make voluntary contributions to her 457 plan, but receives forfeitures in her profit sharing plan, is not considered an active participant.
D. An employee who receives no contributions or forfeitures in her profit sharing plan is not considered an active participant.

78. Which of the following accurately describes the taxation of an annuity owned by a decedent?

A. Accumulated interest is income tax-free.
B. Unpaid interest is considered to be Income in Respect of a Decedent.
C. The decedent's will determines who will receive the proceeds of the annuity.
D. All of the above

79. **Your client recently met with his insurance agent who recommended he purchase an HO-4 policy for his new property. You inform your client that an HO-4 policy has which of the following characteristics?**

    A. It excludes coverage for comprehensive personal liability.
    B. It provides no coverage on the dwelling.
    C. It provides all-risk coverage on personal property.
    D. It provides all-risk coverage on other structures.

80. **The inverse relationship between bond prices and the required rate of return is known as _____**

    A. credit risk.
    B. liquidity risk.
    C. reinvestment risk.
    D. interest rate risk.

81. **Which of the following will shift the Markowitz efficient frontier to the left?**

    A. Taking less risk
    B. Taking more risk
    C. Selecting investments with lower coefficients of correlation between them
    D. Changing the proportion of securities already invested in the portfolio

82. **Evan (AGI of $150,000) donated stock to his university with an FMV of $90,000. He purchased the stock seven months ago for $80,000. What is Evan's maximum allowable charitable contribution for the current year?**

    A. $45,000
    B. $75,000
    C. $80,000
    D. $90,000

83. **Barbara would like to offer a retirement plan to the employees at her small retail store. She's considering either a SIMPLE or a SEP. Which of the following is a possible disadvantage to Barbara if she selects a SEP?**

    A. A SEP must provide for QPSA/QJSA.
    B. Loans are not allowed.
    C. Employer contributions to a SEP are subject to FICA/FUTA withholding.
    D. An employee age 21 or older, earning $6.50 per hour, who works as few as two hours per week and who has done so for three years is eligible to participate in a SEP.

84. **Miriam sold her portfolio of ETFs and is now required to pay 15% tax on the gain. Which of the following must be true?**

    (1) The ETFs were taxed at long-term capital gain rates.
    (2) Miriam's marginal tax bracket was less than 25%.
    (3) Miriam owned the ETFs for more than one year.
    (4) Miriam's marginal tax bracket was 25% or higher.

    A. (1) and (3) only
    B. (3) and (4) only
    C. (1), (2), and (3) only
    D. (1), (3), and (4) only

85. **Your client, an engineer, would like to purchase disability insurance. He's concerned about becoming totally disabled, but also about a reduction in income if he's forced to work fewer hours due to partial disability. To satisfy your client's concerns, which of the following should be included in his disability coverage?**

    A. Cost-of-living adjustment
    B. Waiver of premium
    C. Change-of-occupation provision
    D. Residual disability benefits

For questions 86-89, match the type of group life insurance with the description that follows. Use only one answer per blank. Answers may be used more than once or not at all.

    A. Group survivors' income insurance
    B. Group whole life insurance
    C. Group term life insurance
    D. Group paid-up life insurance
    E. Dependents' group life insurance

86. _____ **Policy that is payable only to an employee's surviving spouse and children**

87. _____ **Combination of two basic plans: accumulating units of permanent life insurance and decreasing units of group term life insurance**

88. _____ **Policy must cover all eligible dependents if the employer pays the entire premium**

89. _____ **Policy that pays a death benefit to the employee's named beneficiary if the employee dies while covered under the policy (A medical exam is usually not required.)**

90. How many continuing education (CE) hours are required per reporting period for a CFP® practitioner to renew her certification?

    A. 10
    B. 20
    C. 30
    D. 40

For questions 91-95, match the type of doctrine with the description that follows. Use only one answer per blank. Answers may be used more than once or not at all.

    A. Substance over form
    B. Hobby-loss rule
    C. Step transaction
    D. Assignment of interest
    E. Constructive receipt
    F. Sham transaction
    G. Assignment of income

91. _____ John owns Apex, Inc., an S Corp. He directs that all income should be paid to his 11-year old son. The father reports no income and the son reports it on his own tax return.

92. _____ Mary assigns her insurance policy as security for a loan.

93. _____ A transaction lacks a business purpose and economic substance, and will therefore be ignored for tax purposes. For example, consider a sale by ABC to LMN, but both ABC and LMN are owned by the same person.

94. _____ Jill owns a participating life insurance policy with dividends accumulating with interest inside the policy.

95. _____ The tax that results from a series of steps in a transaction should be determined based on the overall transaction.

96. **Jameson is self-employed and runs a sole proprietorship. He pays his son $11 per hour to enter sales data into his inventory system. Jameson's son, age 15, will earn $2,200 this year. Which of the following is/ are true regarding the wage Jameson pays to his son?**

    (1) Jameson must withhold FICA taxes
    (2) Jameson must withhold FUTA taxes
    (3) Jameson has to match his son's FICA and FUTA taxes
    (4) Jameson is not required to withhold taxes

    A. (4) only
    B. (1) and (2) only
    C. (1) and (3) only
    D. (1), (2), and (3) only

97. **An investor who expects a large increase in the stock market ninety days from today can take advantage of the change by:**

    A. Buying S&P 500 index puts
    B. Buying S&P 500 index calls
    C. Writing S&P 500 index calls
    D. Both A and C are correct

98. **If property subject to a specific bequest is gifted, lost, or sold prior to the testator's death, the bequest will fail under which of the following doctrines?**

    A. Abatement
    B. Ademption
    C. Rescission
    D. Reformation

99. **Michael recently lost his job and wants to elect COBRA coverage. How long does Michael have before the COBRA election period expires?**

    A. 60 days after Michael's termination date
    B. 60 days after notice of the event was given to Michael by the plan administrator
    C. 30 days after Michael's termination date
    D. 30 days after notice of the event was given to Michael by the plan administrator

100. Which of the following statements about property held as tenancy by entirety are correct?

(1) The property automatically passes to the surviving co-tenant when one tenant dies.
(2) It is an interest in property that can be held only by spouses.
(3) It can be held by non-spouse business partners in an LLC.
(4) In most states, it is not severable by an individual tenant.

A. (1) and (2) only
B. (2) and (4) only
C. (1), (2), and (3) only
D. (1), (2), and (4) only

101. If a portfolio has a beta of 1.0, what type of risk does the portfolio have?

A. Systematic risk
B. Non-systematic risk
C. Diversifiable risk
D. Both non-systematic and diversifiable risk

For questions 102-105, determine what effect the following events will have on a pension plan. Use only one answer per blank. Answers may be used more than once or not at all.

A. Decrease employer contributions
B. Increase employer contributions
C. No effect on employer contributions

102. _____ Forfeitures are not reallocated to remaining participants.

103. _____ A highly compensated employee is replaced by a recent college graduate.

104. _____ Salary levels for all employees decrease as a result of cutbacks.

105. _____ Pension plan investment returns are better than expected.

106. **A large interest rate change has the most significant impact on a _____ bond.**

    A. short duration
    B. high coupon
    C. low coupon
    D. short maturity

107. **Your client would like to set up a revocable living trust but is concerned about potential adverse tax consequences. If he sets up a revocable living trust and places all of his income producing assets into the trust, how will the income from the trust be taxed?**

    A. The income will be taxed at trust tax rates.
    B. The income will pass through to the client, who will pay it personally.
    C. The income will accumulate tax-free within the trust.
    D. Part of the income will pass through to the client, who will pay it personally, and part of the income will accumulate tax-free within the trust.

108. **Bridgeway, Inc. adopts a defined benefit plan with a permitted disparity of 22.50%. Given the permitted disparity, the excess percentage will be _____.**

    A. 22.50%
    B. 26.25%
    C. 45.00%
    D. 48.75%

109. **Mr. Smith entered into a disability and life buy-sell agreement with his business partner, Mr. Jones. Mr. Smith's basis in the business is $200,000 and the buyout is for $1,000,000. How much income will be taxable to Mr. Smith if he becomes disabled or to his family if he dies?**

    A. $0 / $0
    B. $800,000 / $0
    C. $200,000 / $1,000,000
    D. $800,000 / $1,000,000

110. **Assume the return on the stock market is 9.0% and the risk-free rate is 4.5%. What is the stock's risk premium if the beta is 0.8?**

    A. 2.4%
    B. 3.6%
    C. 4.5%
    D. 7.2%

111. **Your client is tax sensitive and wants to pay the least amount of income taxes possible. She's researching various credits and deductions, and asks you which is more beneficial. You tell her:**

    (1) A deduction is more beneficial to a lower-bracket taxpayer.
    (2) A deduction is more beneficial to a higher-bracket taxpayer.
    (3) A credit is more beneficial to a lower-bracket taxpayer.
    (4) A credit is more beneficial to a higher-bracket taxpayer.

    A. (1) and (3) only
    B. (1) and (4) only
    C. (2) and (3) only
    D. (2) and (4) only

112. **Which of the following is true regarding gift splitting?**

    A. A married couple can select which gifts made during the year will receive split gift treatment.
    B. A gift made after one spouse dies can still be split.
    C. The split gift election is commonly used with community property.
    D. When the gift splitting election is made, gifts made by either spouse are treated as being made one-half by each spouse.

113. **Which of the following options will put an investor at the greatest risk?**

    A. Selling a stock short while not owning the stock
    B. Selling a stock short while owning the stock
    C. Buying a put while not owning the stock
    D. Buying a put while owning the stock

114. Paul would like to leave the majority of his estate to his daughter, Claire. All but which of the following provisions in Paul's will would affect how much Claire will receive when he dies?

    A. The tax clause
    B. The attestation clause
    C. The debts clause
    D. The residuary clause

115. Which of the following is the correct reason to purchase a particular investment for a client's portfolio?

    A. Growth stocks because they pay high dividends
    B. FNMA securities because they are backed by the full faith and credit of the US government
    C. A global fund because it provides only international exposure
    D. Blue chip common stocks because they provide a hedge against inflation

116. Which of the following accounts is most appropriate for a zero-coupon bond?

    A. Payable on death account
    B. IRA
    C. Joint taxable account
    D. Totten trust

117. Which of the following would be the most authoritative and would carry the highest precedential value in defending a client's tax position against the IRS?

    A. Procedural regulation
    B. Revenue ruling
    C. Treasury regulation
    D. Technical advice memoranda

118. A life insurance policy that pays a dividend is known as a _____

    A. noncancellable policy.
    B. participating policy.
    C. non-participating policy.
    D. return of premium policy.

119. **Which of the following retirement plans are subject to the Pension Benefit Guaranty Corporation (PBGC)?**

(1) Age-weighted profit sharing plan
(2) Target benefit plan
(3) Cash balance plan
(4) SARSEP

A. (3) only
B. (1) and (2) only
C. (1) and (3) only
D. (3) and (4) only

120. **An investor concerned that a stock he owns will soon decrease substantially in value should choose which of the following options?**

A. Buy a call
B. Sell a call
C. Buy a put
D. Sell a put

121. **Each year Ben rents out his beachfront home in Myrtle Beach to college students during spring break. Ben charges $4,000 per week, and the total rental period is 14 days. Which of the following is true?**

A. The repairs are deductible, but Ben is not permitted to show a loss.
B. Ben can deduct the repairs he'll have to pay against his income.
C. In addition to deducting repair costs, Ben can deduct a portion of his real estate taxes, depreciation, and other related expenses.
D. Ben doesn't have to report the $8,000 income.

122. **For an IRA owner born after June 30, what is her age for the purposes of calculating her first required minimum distribution?**

A. Age 70
B. Age 71
C. Split between age 70 and 71
D. The IRA owner is permitted to select age 70 or 71.

123. All of the following are elements of an insurable risk, except:

A. The loss must be due to chance.
B. The severity and frequency of the loss are determinants of risk treatment.
C. There must be a large number of homogeneous exposure units to make losses reasonably predictable.
D. The loss must be definite and measurable.

124. Which of the following is preferred by a risk-averse investor?

A. Low kurtosis
B. Mid kurtosis
C. High kurtosis
D. Kurtosis is insignificant

125. Which of the following is true regarding a qualified domestic trust (QDOT)?

A. There must be at least one trustee who is a US citizen or a qualifying domestic corporation.
B. The surviving spouse must have the right to all income, as well as a general power of appointment over trust assets.
C. The trust does not qualify for the marital deduction unless a special election is made by the trustee.
D. Property in the trust is not subject to gift or estate taxes.

126. Susan owned ABC stock with a basis of $10 per share. At the time of her death, the stock was worth $25 per share. Six months later, the stock was valued at $35 per share. What is the basis of the stock in the hands of Susan's beneficiary?

A. $10
B. $15
C. $25
D. $35

127. **Meridian, Inc., a C Corp, had a profitable year and now has extra money to invest. The owners would like to maximize the after-tax income to the corporation. Which of the following investments would you recommend?**

    A. Value stocks
    B. Preferred stock
    C. Municipal bonds
    D. Highly-rated corporate bonds

128. **Steve Pascal, an individual taxpayer, donated $40,000 to the Red Cross last year when his gross income was $75,000. This year, when Steve's gross income is $80,000, he makes no donations to charity. How much of Steve's $40,000 gift is he allowed to deduct?**

    A. Last year: $22,500 / This year: $0
    B. Last year: $22,500 / This year: $17,500
    C. Last year: $37,500 / This year: $0
    D. Last year: $37,500 / This year: $2,500

129. **Marie, a single taxpayer with an AGI of $140,000, is permitted to make a fully deductible IRA contribution if she's an active participant in which of the following plans?**

    A. 401k with no match
    B. 403b with no match
    C. 403b with match
    D. 457

130. **Which of the following organizations is not permitted to establish a 403b plan for its employees?**

    A. Private school
    B. State government
    C. Public school
    D. Federal government

131. Jessica, age 67, recently received a $650,000 inheritance from her uncle's estate. To provide sufficient income during retirement, she needs an annuity that will produce the highest payout for the rest of her life. Which settlement option should Jessica select?

    A. Dollar certain
    B. Joint life
    C. Single life
    D. Life with a 10-year period certain

132. Ryan works as an independent contractor to teach golf lessons at the local country club. Which of the following taxes will Ryan have to pay?

    (1) Income taxes
    (2) Medicare payroll taxes
    (3) Social security payroll taxes

    A. (1) only
    B. (1) and (3) only
    C. (2) and (3) only
    D. All of the above

133. Your client, Dr. Auld, needs more life insurance but insists on purchasing a participating policy. Which of the following characteristics of participating policies should you point out to Dr. Auld?

    A. Insurers are allowed to guarantee future dividends for a maximum of two years.
    B. Only stock insurance companies can issue policies that pay dividends.
    C. Any dividends paid will be fully tax deductible to Dr. Auld.
    D. Policy dividends are partly a return of a deliberate overcharge of premium by the insurer.

134. Which of the following statements accurately describes a variable life insurance policy?

    A. Premiums and death benefits are both flexible.
    B. It is made up of increasing units of term insurance and a guaranteed cash value.
    C. A minimum death benefit is guaranteed.
    D. The death benefit is linked to the performance of the S&P 500 only.

135. **Which of the following describes the conversion provision in a life insurance policy?**

    A. The insured may purchase additional amounts of insurance without having to complete a medical exam.
    B. The insured is guaranteed the right to exchange term insurance for permanent insurance, but only if he or she faces long-term disability.
    C. The insured may convert from permanent insurance to term insurance without having to show evidence of insurability.
    D. The insured may convert from term insurance to permanent insurance without having to show evidence of insurability.

136. **Stanley, a CFP® practitioner, is registered with the SEC as an investment adviser through his financial planning firm, Pinnacle Advisors. Which of the following statements is correct?**

    A. Stanley may use the initials "RIA" on his marketing brochures.
    B. Stanley must use the words "Registered Investment Adviser" after his name.
    C. Stanley must disclose his firm's status as a registered investment adviser.
    D. Stanley may use the initials "R.I.A." on his business cards.

137. **A modified endowment contract (MEC) has all of the following characteristics, except:**

    A. Meets the "seven-pay test"
    B. Meets the requirements of a life insurance contract
    C. Fails to meet the guideline premium and corridor test
    D. Was entered into after 6/21/88

138. **Your client owns shares of a closely held C Corp and read an article in the *Wall Street Journal* about a possible reduction in estate taxes he may be entitled to. The Code section your client is referring to is** _____

    A. section 6166.
    B. section 303.
    C. section 2503(c).
    D. section 2032(a).

139. All of the following are correct regarding a Rabbi trust, except:

A. The trust may include a bankruptcy trigger.
B. The trust may become irrevocable if there is a change in corporate control.
C. Corporate assets may be contributed to the trust.
D. The trust creates security for employees because the assets within the trust are outside the employer's control.

140. Which of the following will increase an employer's contribution to a defined benefit plan?

(1) Lower than expected investment returns
(2) High turnover among employees
(3) High ratio of married to unmarried participants
(4) Large forfeitures

A. (1) and (2) only
B. (1) and (3) only
C. (2) and (3) only
D. (3) and (4) only

141. Which of the following statements is true regarding a typical whole life insurance policy?

A. The cash value cannot be used to provide collateral for a loan.
B. The difference between a policy's face amount and the reserve must be greater than the cash surrender value at all times.
C. The cash value must equal the face amount of coverage by the end of the mortality table.
D. The premiums must be paid for the insured's entire lifetime, or for a period of at least ten years.

142. Which of the following stock market anomalies support the efficient market hypothesis?

(1) The Neglected Stock Effect
(2) The Value Line Anomaly
(3) The January Effect
(4) The Turn-of-the-Month Effect

A. (1) and (3) only
B. (2) and (3) only
C. None of the above
D. All of the above

143. **Your client has a private annuity and asks you what impact this will have on the value of her gross estate at death. You tell her the value of her private annuity is:**

    A. Treated the same as an installment sale
    B. Valued at its FMV on the date of death
    C. Valued at its FMV on the alternate valuation date
    D. Not included in her gross estate

144. **After reading an article in *Money Magazine*, your client asks you to explain the difference between open-end and closed-end mutual funds. You tell him that open-end mutual funds have which of the following characteristics?**

    (1) They sell at their net asset value.
    (2) They may sell at a discount from their net asset value.
    (3) They issue new stock whenever an individual buys shares.
    (4) They have a fixed capital structure.

    A. (1) and (3) only
    B. (1) and (4) only
    C. (2) and (3) only
    D. (2) and (4) only

145. **Larry Minor recently made his annual IRA contribution. Which of the following investments is he permitted to purchase within his IRA?**

    (1) Money market funds
    (2) Stocks
    (3) Mutual funds
    (4) Real estate

    A. (1) and (3) only
    B. (2) and (3) only
    C. (1), (2) and (3) only
    D. All of the above

146. Stephanie bought a call option for $2.00. The option has a strike price of $22.00, and the stock is currently trading at $21.50. The call option would cost $1.50 if purchased today. What is the intrinsic value of Stephanie's option?

A. - $0.50
B. $0
C. $0.50
D. $2.00

147. John read an article about "alternative investments" and the benefits they provide investors. One benefit that John particularly liked was their low correlation with the US stock market. John decided to buy a rare antique in his IRA because he thought it would be considered an alternative investment. What is John's penalty, if any, for purchasing an antique inside his IRA?

A. The antique is considered an investment. Any income generated from the sale of the antique will be tax-free income to John.
B. The purchase of the antique will be considered a nondeductible contribution in the year of purchase.
C. The purchase of the antique will be considered an excess contribution in the year of purchase.
D. The purchase of the antique will be considered a distribution from the IRA in the year of purchase.

148. Your client is interested in purchasing a long-term care insurance policy and asks you to explain the potential benefits and drawbacks of this type of coverage. You tell him that long-term care insurance has which of the following characteristics?

(1) Covered care can be provided only in a hospital or skilled nursing care facility.
(2) Coverage must be provided for at least twelve months.
(3) Buying a policy is usually not necessary because Medicare will provide adequate protection when the individual turns age 65.

A. (1) only
B. (2) only
C. (1) and (3) only
D. (2) and (3) only

149. Which of the following variables are used to calculate a stock's beta coefficient?

(1) The standard deviation of the return for a particular security
(2) The correlation coefficient between the return for a particular security and the return for the overall market
(3) The standard deviation of the return for the overall market

A. (2) only
B. (3) only
C. (1) and (3) only
D. All of the above

150. Regarding estate and gift tax laws, which of the following is not subject to an adjustment for inflation?

A. GSTT annual exclusion
B. Applicable credit amount
C. Special use value reduction
D. Gift tax annual exclusion

151. Mike Shapiro owns RGWN, Inc., an S Corp. Mike started the company five years ago with $45,000 cash. Due to unforeseen business problems, he lent the company another $20,000 to stay in operation. For the year, RGWN, Inc. had a net operating loss of $100,000. How much can Mike deduct as a loss on his tax return?

A. $20,000
B. $45,000
C. $65,000
D. $100,000

For questions 152-155, match the charitable trust with the description that follows. Use only one answer per blank. Answers may be used more than once or not at all.

    A. Charitable remainder annuity trust (CRAT)
    B. Charitable remainder unitrust (CRUT)
    C. Neither A or B
    D. Both A and B

152. ____ Income tax savings, income is a sum certain

153. ____ Income tax savings, income can be provided for life

154. ____ Income tax savings, immediate income to charity

155. ____ Estate tax savings, income is variable

156. Rob purchased an art sculpture for $8,000. Years later, when the sculpture was worth $3,000, he gave it to his brother, Bill, as a gift. Nine months later, Bill sold the sculpture at auction for $2,000. Assuming Bill paid no gift taxes on the sculpture when he received it, what was his net gain or loss on the sale?

    A. $1,000 loss
    B. $2,000 gain
    C. $6,000 loss
    D. $0 gain, $0 loss

157. Dr. Krier would like to learn more about the tax benefits of having a home office. He's come to you for advice. You tell him which of the following statements are true concerning a home office?

(1) The costs associated with running a home office can be expensed by Dr. Krier if he uses the office primarily for business.

(2) Dr. Krier's home office must be either his principal place of business, or where he meets with patients in the normal course of business.

(3) If Dr. Krier uses a separate structure not attached to his home for an exclusive and regular part of his business, he can deduct the expenses related to it.

(4) The home office deduction can generate a loss to be used against income from Dr. Krier's other activities.

A. (1) and (2) only
B. (1) and (3) only
C. (2) and (3) only
D. (2) and (4) only

158. Profit sharing plans have which of the following characteristics?

A. They favor older employees.
B. They can be invested entirely in company stock.
C. They are a type of defined contribution pension plan.
D. The minimum funding standard requires the employer to make an annual contribution.

159. Which of the following are considered taxable income?

(1) Alimony
(2) Child support
(3) Workers compensation
(4) Premiums paid by an employer on $100,000 of group term life insurance

A. (1) and (2) only
B. (1) and (4) only
C. (2) and (3) only
D. (1), (3), and (4) only

160. **How is the value of publicly traded stocks and bonds determined for gift and estate tax purposes?**

   A. The closing price on the date of disposition
   B. The opening price on the date of disposition
   C. The mean between the highest and lowest selling price on the date of disposition
   D. The mean between the highest and lowest selling price on the date prior to the date of disposition

161. **Brian transferred assets to an irrevocable trust for the benefit of his two daughters, Carol and Kate. Brian will be taxed on income from the trust if he retains which of the following powers?**

   A. The power to sprinkle income between Carol and Kate
   B. The power to add his nephew as a beneficiary
   C. The power to accumulate income within the trust while Carol and Kate are under age 18
   D. The power to invade the trust principal for Carol and Kate's health, education, maintenance, and support (HEMS)

162. **Which of the following interests can be disclaimed by a beneficiary?**

   (1) A beneficiary's income interest in a revocable living trust
   (2) A beneficiary's right to the death benefit from a universal life insurance policy
   (3) A beneficiary's remainder interest in an irrevocable trust
   (4) A joint tenant's survivorship interest in a boat

   A. (1) and (3) only
   B. (1) and (4) only
   C. (2) and (3) only
   D. All of the above

163. **Which of the following is an advantage that money purchase plans have over other qualified retirement plans?**

   A. They are easy to explain to employees.
   B. They favor older employees.
   C. Forfeitures must be used to reduce future employer contributions.
   D. Employer contributions can be omitted in bad years and must only be substantial and recurring.

164. Which of the following will qualify as alimony?

   A. The wife pays the mortgage for the home owned by her husband as specified in a written separation agreement.
   B. The ex-wife transfers an investment property to her ex-husband as specified in the divorce decree.
   C. During the time the spouses are separated before their divorce, the husband makes auto loan payments on behalf of his wife.
   D. The ex-husband makes a payment of $650 per month to his ex-wife until their child reaches age 18, pursuant to the divorce decree.

165. Your client is tax sensitive and concerned about having to pay AMT. You tell him which of the following are tax preference items or adjustments for AMT?

   (1) Interest earned on general obligation municipal bonds
   (2) The bargain element of ISOs
   (3) The difference between accelerated depreciation and straight line depreciation on a piece of property
   (4) The interest expense on an investment property in excess of investment income

   A. (1) and (3) only
   B. (1) and (4) only
   C. (2) and (3) only
   D. (1), (2), and (3) only

For questions 166-169, select the power of appointment that is appropriate for the scenario given. Use only one answer per blank. Answers may be used more than once or not at all.

   A. Special power of appointment
   B. General power of appointment
   C. Neither a special power nor a general power of appointment
   D. Both a special power and a general power of appointment

166. _____ The power to appoint funds held by another entity

167. _____ When the holder dies, assets are includible in her gross estate.

168. _____ The power to appoint assets to oneself that can be exercised only with the consent of an adverse party.

169. _____ A holder's release of the power causes a gift for federal gift tax purposes.

170. A fixed income security is subject to which of the following risks?

(1) Exchange rate risk
(2) Purchasing power risk
(3) Default risk
(4) Liquidity risk
(5) Reinvestment rate risk

A. (1), (2), (3), and (4) only
B. (1), (2), (4), and (5) only
C. (2), (3), (4), and (5) only
D. All of the above

171. Which of the following estate planning objectives can be accomplished through a will?

A. Provide for decisions during incapacitation
B. Establish a testamentary credit shelter trust
C. Avoid probate
D. Provide burial wishes

172. Your client is confused about the difference between a will and a living will. You tell her that a living will has which of the following characteristics?

A. Allows an individual to appoint property before death
B. Allows an individual to specify wishes about medical treatment and artificial life support under specific circumstances
C. Has the same function as a revocable living trust
D. All of the above

173. Which of the following debts may be discharged through bankruptcy court?

(1) Auto loans
(2) Alimony
(3) Government loans
(4) Child support
(5) Credit card debt

A. (1) and (5) only
B. (2) and (4) only
C. (1), (2), and (5) only
D. (2), (3), and (4) only

174. Your client, age 56, recently lost his job and feels the only way he can support his family is to make withdrawals from his IRA. You inform your client that in limited circumstances the 10% early withdrawal penalty does not apply. Which of the following are among the exemptions from the 10% penalty?

(1) Higher education costs for the participant's child
(2) Hardship withdrawals
(3) First-time home purchase up to $10,000
(4) Separation from service at age 55 or older
(5) Loan for medical expenses

A. (1) and (3) only
B. (2) and (4) only
C. (3) and (5) only
D. (1), (3), and (4) only

175. Your client purchased a limited pay whole life insurance policy ten years ago. He recently lost his job and can no longer afford to pay the premium. However, he continues to need life insurance. Which of the following is a non-forfeiture option your client can select?

A. Paid-up reduced amount
B. Life annuity
C. Paid-up additions
D. Accumulate with interest

176. Johnny, age 13, works for his father developing children's computer programs. His father owns and operates a sole proprietorship. Johnny is paid $10,000 per year for his work. What is Johnny's tax bracket for the majority of his earnings?

A. Johnny's own tax bracket with a reduction for social security
B. Johnny's own tax bracket without a reduction for social security
C. His father's marginal tax bracket with a reduction for social security
D. His father's marginal tax bracket without a reduction for social security

177. Which of the following is an advantage an S Corp holds over a personal service corporation (PSC)?

    A. S Corps provide a step-up in basis at death; PSCs do not.
    B. S Corps pass through earnings and losses; PSCs do not.
    C. S Corps provide limited liability; PSCs do not.
    D. S Corps allow deductions for business expenses; PSCs do not.

178. Your client, Ben Gibbons, buys two puts:
August LMN put at $36, currently selling at $38
December XYZ put at $29, currently selling at $26
Ignoring transaction costs, what is the intrinsic value of Ben's options?

    A. LMN: -$2 / XYZ: $0
    B. LMN: -$2 / XYZ: $3
    C. LMN: $0 / XYZ: -$3
    D. LMN: $0 / XYZ: $3

179. Which of the following is eligible for a like-kind exchange?

    A. Business equipment
    B. Stocks and bonds
    C. Different sex livestock
    D. Inventory held in a warehouse

180. Amos Tupper, age 63, is retired and wants to receive his social security benefits 36 months early. His normal retirement age is 66. How much will Amos' social security benefit be reduced?

    A. 15%
    B. 20%
    C. 25%
    D. There will be no reduction if Amos is retired.

181. **An actuary is required to establish and/or administer which of the following retirement plans?**

    (1) Target benefit plan
    (2) Profit sharing plan
    (3) Money purchase plan
    (4) Defined benefit plan

    A. (4) only
    B. (1) and (4) only
    C. (2) and (4) only
    D. (3) and (4) only

182. **Your client, Chris Norris, sells a naked call on Google for a $250 premium. Which of the following is true about Chris' position?**

    A. Chris is expecting Google stock to increase in value.
    B. Chris' potential loss is unlimited.
    C. Chris' potential loss is limited to $250.
    D. Chris' outlook for Google stock is bullish.

183. **A participant in a defined contribution plan is least affected by which of the following factors?**

    A. Investment performance
    B. Life expectancy
    C. Pre-retirement inflation
    D. Account balance

184. **On August 5 of last year, Joel bought 250 shares of Dell stock for $35 per share. On December 30 of last year, he sold all 250 shares for $6,250. On January 20 of this year, Joel bought back 250 shares of Dell stock for $35 per share. What is the result of Joel's transaction?**

    A. If Joel waited a few more days to buy back the stock, he could have realized the gain.
    B. Joel can realize the $2,500 loss.
    C. The wash sale rule doesn't apply to a dealer in securities.
    D. No loss deduction is allowed; the amount of the disallowed loss will be added to the cost basis of the shares Joel purchased on January 20.

185. Your client sold a piece of land to her church for $400,000. The FMV of the land at the time of sale was $800,000. Your client's original basis in the land was $200,000. What is the taxable gain resulting from the sale?

    A. $0
    B. $200,000
    C. $300,000
    D. $400,000

186. Target benefit plans share which of the following characteristics with defined benefit plans?

    (1) Individual account balances are used to record the financial status of each participant.
    (2) Contributions are determined through actuarial calculations.

    A. (1) only
    B. (2) only
    C. None of the above
    D. All of the above

187. Mr. and Mrs. Stern are interested in creating a family budget. During the data gathering phase, you discover their prior budgets have failed because they didn't follow the proper budgeting process. You tell them the first step of the budgeting process is:

    A. List all categories and amounts of fixed expenses.
    B. Determine how much needs to be saved.
    C. Estimate all income and sources of income.
    D. List all categories and amounts of discretionary expenses.

188. Grady and Donna Fletcher have a daughter, age 18, who is preparing to start college in the Fall. Although Grady and Donna earn a high income, they do not have adequate college savings already set aside and will need a loan. However, due to their high income, they won't qualify for a needs-based program. As their financial planner, you recommend they consider which of the following?

(1) Perkins Loan
(2) 529 Plan
(3) Parent Loan for Undergraduate Students (PLUS)
(4) Subsidized Stafford student loan

A. (1) and (2) only
B. (1) and (4) only
C. (2) and (3) only
D. (2) and (4) only

189. The principle of indemnity is enforced in which of the following ways?

A. Through the principle of subrogation
B. To a greater extent in disability insurance than in property and casualty insurance
C. Through a specific rider or endorsement
D. Through policy laws

190. Ryan has owned his company, Golf Solutions, for 17 years. He is now 52 years old and plans to retire at age 64. He has five young employees and wants to set up a retirement plan that will provide him with the highest benefit. Assuming adequate cash flow, the most suitable plan for Golf Solutions is a/an _____

A. money purchase plan.
B. defined benefit plan.
C. SIMPLE IRA.
D. age-based profit sharing plan.

191. **Which of the following miscellaneous itemized deductions are not subject to the 2% of AGI floor?**

    A. Professional and business association dues
    B. Costs of looking for a new job
    C. Work uniforms not suitable for regular wear
    D. Gambling losses to the extent of winnings

192. **Your client is concerned about maintaining her privacy, even at death. She would like to avoid probate. Which of the following methods of titling property will allow her to achieve her goal?**

    (1) JTWROS
    (2) Tenancy in common
    (3) Totten trust
    (4) Tenancy by entirety
    (5) Payable on death provision
    (6) Community property

    A. (2) and (6) only
    B. (1), (4), and (5) only
    C. (1), (3), (4), and (5) only
    D. (1), (3), (4), (5), and (6) only

193. **Charlie will begin receiving social security benefits this year. You inform Charlie that a portion of his benefits may be taxable. Which of the following will be added to Charlie's AGI to determine the taxation of his benefits?**

    (1) Unemployment income
    (2) Charlie's salary
    (3) Workers compensation
    (4) General obligation municipal bond interest

    A. (1), (2), and (3) only
    B. (1), (2), and (4) only
    C. (1), (3), and (4) only
    D. (2), (3), and (4) only

194. Which of the following is the penalty for failing to file a tax return?

    A. 75% of the underpayment
    B. 5% of the tax due per month, up to a maximum of 25%
    C. 0.5% of the unpaid tax per month, up to a maximum of 25%
    D. 20% of the underpayment

195. Your client is interested in providing group term life insurance to the employees at his engineering firm. However, he would first like to understand the tax impact this will have on him as the employer, as well as for his employees. You tell him that employer-provided group term life insurance has which of the following characteristics?

    (1) The cost for up to $50,000 of coverage is tax-free to each employee.
    (2) An employer can deduct its contribution to a group life insurance plan even if it pays for $150,000 of coverage.

    A. (1) only
    B. (2) only
    C. None of the above
    D. All of the above

196. Two years ago, your client was granted incentive stock options (ISOs) by her employer and she would like to exercise them. She asks you what tax impact, if any, this will have. You tell her that incentive stock options are subject to the following taxes at the time of exercise:

    (1) AMT
    (2) FICA

    A. (1) only
    B. (2) only
    C. None of the above
    D. All of the above

197. **Your client has been given an unfunded deferred compensation plan by his employer as a reward for his ten years of service. Which of the following statements concerning the tax treatment of his benefit payments is correct?**

(1) All payments will be taxed as ordinary income when received.
(2) All payments will be subject to social security taxes.

A. (1) only
B. (2) only
C. None of the above
D. All of the above

198. **Pete participates in his company's ESOP plan. The company initially transferred 1,000 shares of stock into Pete's account. Four years later, when the stock was worth $10 per share, Pete retired. If he elected to receive the stock at retirement and sells it today (six years later) for $15,000, what are the tax consequences?**

A. $3,000 ordinary income at distribution, $12,000 capital gain
B. $10,000 ordinary income at distribution, $5,000 capital gain
C. $12,000 ordinary income at distribution, $3,000 capital gain
D. $15,000 capital gain at time of sale

199. **When property is transferred for less than full consideration of money or money's worth, the value of the gift is equal to which of the following?**

A. The value of the property transferred plus the consideration received
B. The value of the consideration received
C. The lesser of the value of the property or the consideration received
D. The value of the property transferred less the consideration received

200. John Miller, age 56, recently retired from Harbor, Inc., and would like to take his family on an expensive cruise around the world. He'll need to take a distribution from a retirement plan to pay for the trip. Which of the following plans would allow John to take a penalty free withdrawal?

A. Single premium deferred annuity
B. Traditional IRA
C. Money purchase plan from his employer before Harbor, Inc.
D. 401k from Harbor, Inc.

201. Which of the following are included in the probate estate?

(1) A transferable on death account between the decedent and his grandchild
(2) A condo owned JTWROS
(3) A home owned as community property
(4) A general power of appointment held by the decedent
(5) An insurance policy owned by the decedent (spouse is the insured)
(6) An IRA without a beneficiary designation

A. (1), (2), and (4) only
B. (2), (4), and (6) only
C. (3), (5), and (6) only
D. (3), (4), (5), and (6) only

202. All of the following statements regarding bonds and preferred stock are correct, except:

A. If a company declares bankruptcy, bond holders are repaid before preferred stock shareholders.
B. Preferred stocks pay dividends; bonds pay interest.
C. Bonds are subject to greater interest rate risk than preferred stock.
D. Neither bond interest nor preferred stock dividends qualify for capital gains treatment.

For questions 203-207, match each security description with the appropriate term that follows. Use only one answer per blank. Answers may be used more than once or not at all.

A. Freely traded in secondary markets; yield and term are determined at the time of purchase

B. Pay a fixed rate of interest every six months until maturity; issued in terms of ten years or more

C. Can be redeemed at any time without penalty; objective is to earn interest for shareholders

D. Unsecured promissory note issued by corporations with a fixed maturity of up to 270 days

E. Intended to be held until maturity, but can be redeemed prior to maturity for a penalty

F. Dividends are declared in local currencies and paid in US dollars

203. _____ **Money market funds**

204. _____ **Certificate of deposit**

205. _____ **Commercial paper**

206. _____ **Treasury bonds**

207. _____ **American Depository Receipts**

208. **A mutual fund that invests only in securities outside the US is known as a/an _____**

   A. balanced fund.
   B. international fund.
   C. global fund.
   D. aggressive growth fund.

209. Your client's insurance agent recommends she purchase a universal life insurance policy. She's come to you for a second opinion, and asks you to explain the basic provisions of a universal life policy. You tell her that such policies have the following characteristics:

(1) Flexible premium
(2) Unbundled structure
(3) Flexible death benefit
(4) Minimum guaranteed cash value

A. (2) only
B. (1) and (3) only
C. (1), (2), and (3) only
D. (1), (3), and (4) only

For questions 210-215, match the step of the financial planning process with the description that follows. Use only one answer per blank. Answers may be used more than once or not at all.

A. Interview the client; use a fact-finding questionnaire.
B. Assist the client as needed to carry out the recommended plan.
C. Determine the duration of the engagement.
D. Select suitable strategies for goal achievement and recommend them to the client.
E. Determine the client's financial status.
F. Review changes in the client's circumstances and evaluate the performance of the plan.

210. _____ Establishing and defining the client-planner relationship

211. _____ Gathering client data, including goals

212. _____ Analyzing and evaluating the client's financial status

213. _____ Developing and presenting recommendations and/or alternatives

214. _____ Implementing the financial planning recommendations

215. _____ Monitoring the financial plan

For questions 216-220, match the form of dividend with the description that follows. Use only one answer per blank. Answers may be used more than once or not at all.

A. Stock dividend
B. Taxable distribution
C. Ordinary dividend
D. Qualified dividend
E. Constructive dividend
F. Liquidating dividend
G. Stock right

216. _____ A distribution made by a corporation that is paid as additional shares of stock rather than cash

217. _____ A type of dividend to which capital gain tax rates are applied

218. _____ Normally a disguised dividend, such as a below-market shareholder loan

219. _____ A payment to shareholders that exceeds the company's retained earnings; payment is made from capital rather than earnings

220. _____ Ability to subscribe to additional shares of stock at a set price

221. Your elderly client is tax sensitive and wants to pay the least amount of estate taxes at death. Which of the following techniques can he use to reduce his gross estate, and therefore, reduce his estate taxes?

(1) Living trust
(2) Family limited partnership
(3) QPRT
(4) Totten trust

A. (1) and (2) only
B. (2) and (3) only
C. (2) and (4) only
D. (1), (3), and (4) only

222. **Your client received a tip from his accountant about the tax advantages of a QPRT. He asks you for more details, along with your recommendation. You tell him which of the following is/are true regarding a QPRT?**

(1) A QPRT is ideal for a single parent in his 30s or 40s.
(2) A QPRT is generally appropriate for vacation homes valued at over $1,000,000.
(3) After the trust term ends, the house reverts back to the grantor.
(4) The grantor will have a taxable gift upon the creation of a QPRT.

A. (2) only
B. (1) and (2) only
C. (2) and (4) only
D. (1), (3), and (4) only

223. **According to the Rule of 72, how many years will it take for an investment to double if the rate of return is 6% per year?**

A. 10 years
B. 12 years
C. 14 years
D. 16 years

224. **Liability insurance is primarily concerned with which of the following?**

A. Fraud
B. Tax evasion
C. Intentional torts
D. Unintentional torts

225. **Which of the following are differences between ISOs and NSOs?**

(1) Tax treatment at the time of grant
(2) Tax treatment at the time of exercise
(3) Tax treatment at the time of sale

A. (1) only
B. (2) only
C. (3) only
D. (2) and (3) only

ANSWER SHEET

Question	Your Answer	Correct Answer	Notes
1			
2			
3			
4			
5			
6			
7			
8			
9			
10			
11			
12			
13			
14			
15			
16			
17			
18			
19			
20			
21			
22			
23			
24			
25			

NOTES:

Question	Your Answer	Correct Answer	Notes
26			
27			
28			
29			
30			
31			
32			
33			
34			
35			
36			
37			
38			
39			
40			
41			
42			
43			
44			
45			
46			
47			
48			
49			
50			

NOTES:

Question	Your Answer	Correct Answer	Notes
51			
52			
53			
54			
55			
56			
57			
58			
59			
60			
61			
62			
63			
64			
65			
66			
67			
68			
69			
70			
71			
72			
73			
74			
75			

NOTES:

Question	Your Answer	Correct Answer	Notes
76			
77			
78			
79			
80			
81			
82			
83			
84			
85			
86			
87			
88			
89			
90			
91			
92			
93			
94			
95			
96			
97			
98			
99			
100			

NOTES:

Question	Your Answer	Correct Answer	Notes
101			
102			
103			
104			
105			
106			
107			
108			
109			
110			
111			
112			
113			
114			
115			
116			
117			
118			
119			
120			
121			
122			
123			
124			
125			

NOTES:

Question	Your Answer	Correct Answer	Notes
126			
127			
128			
129			
130			
131			
132			
133			
134			
135			
136			
137			
138			
139			
140			
141			
142			
143			
144			
145			
146			
147			
148			
149			
150			

NOTES:

Question	Your Answer	Correct Answer	Notes
151			
152			
153			
154			
155			
156			
157			
158			
159			
160			
161			
162			
163			
164			
165			
166			
167			
168			
169			
170			
171			
172			
173			
174			
175			

NOTES:

Question	Your Answer	Correct Answer	Notes
176			
177			
178			
179			
180			
181			
182			
183			
184			
185			
186			
187			
188			
189			
190			
191			
192			
193			
194			
195			
196			
197			
198			
199			
200			

NOTES:

Question	Your Answer	Correct Answer	Notes
201			
202			
203			
204			
205			
206			
207			
208			
209			
210			
211			
212			
213			
214			
215			
216			
217			
218			
219			
220			
221			
222			
223			
224			
225			

NOTES:

ANSWER KEY

1. C

A sole proprietorship does not limit your client's liability, and is therefore not appropriate. A limited partnership may be suitable, but there is no mention of a general partner. A C Corp would not provide flow-through taxation as your client requested. The best answer is the S Corp.

2. B

The nondeductible excise tax for over-contributing to an IRA is 6%, not 10%. An employee who makes voluntary contributions to a retirement plan is considered an active participant. However, an employee participating in a 457 plan is not an active participant.

3. C

During the third step of the financial planning process, the financial planner will identify the client's financial strengths and weaknesses, and consider available options for the achievement of goals.

4. D

Itemized deductions are personal expenses, such as home mortgage interest and medical expenses that are permitted as a deduction from AGI in arriving at taxable income. They are below-the-line deductions.

5. D

R^2 is the Coefficient of Determination and a measure of systematic risk. If R^2 is high (>0.60), then beta is the relevant measure to use when comparing securities. The beta measures are Jensen's alpha and Treynor. If R^2 is low (<0.60), then standard deviation is the relevant measure to use when comparing securities. The standard deviation measure is Sharpe.

6. C

By using a beneficiary or joint tenancy, assets will pass by contract and avoid probate. Even though the assets will not be included in her probate estate, they will still be included in her gross estate. Life insurance payable to a decedent's estate is subject to probate.

7. C

In a conditionally renewable policy, the insurer has the right not to renew the policy for specific reasons listed in the contract.

8. A

A noncancellable policy gives the insured the right to renew for a stated number of years, with a guaranteed premium at renewal.

9. D

A guaranteed renewable policy gives the insured the right to renew for a stated number of years. The insurer cannot change the premium unless the change is made for an entire class of policyholders.

10. C

The defined benefit plan, target benefit plan, and cash balance plan all favor older employees. Money purchase plans guarantee a contribution will be made each year, and will help Dr. Bowman achieve his goal.

11. B

Mike's loss is limited to $50 per credit card. However, one card has only $25 charged against it, so his loss is limited to only $25 for that card.

12. B

To make a valid S Corp election, all shareholders must be US citizens, or residents, or a qualifying trust. All shareholders must consent to the S Corp election, not just the majority. There may be no more than 100 shareholders, and there may only be one class of stock.

13. C

CAPM determines the required rate of return for a stock based on its beta and the stock market's overall rate of return. That rate of return is then used in the dividend growth model to value common stock.

14. D

Peggy can contribute more than 25% to an individual employee's account, but the contributions must remain under the IRC Section 415 limit. The total company contributions cannot exceed 25% of total plan compensation.

15. B

A payable on death account is included in the gross estate but avoids probate.

16. A

An IRA without a named beneficiary is included in the gross estate and goes through probate. If the IRA had a named beneficiary, it would be included in the gross estate but would avoid probate.

17. A

An apartment building held as tenancy in common is included in the gross estate and goes through probate.

18. A
A restaurant owned by the decedent is included in the gross estate and goes through probate. Because no property titling is provided in the question, we must assume the restaurant is held in its simplest form as a sole proprietorship.

19. B
A bank account held as tenancy by entirety is included in the gross estate but avoids probate.

20. D
A testamentary trust has no effect.

21. A
A home held as community property is included in the gross estate and goes through probate.

22. D
The deductibility of long-term care premiums depends on the insured's age. The premiums are not deductible in full.

23. D
Index mutual funds can only be purchased at the end of the trading day. ETFs carry low management fees because once they are created, there's very little management needed. There is a transaction fee any time an ETF is bought or sold.

24. C
The monthly parking allowance, sporting event tickets, and group disability benefits are tax-free fringe benefits. The allowable discount for services (dental work) is limited to 20% of the price at which the employer offers services to non-employees.

25. A
In a defined contribution plan, the employee is responsible for the investment performance. The contributions made by the employer must be defined, and benefits cannot be provided for past service. In a defined benefit plan, the employer assumes the risk of pre-retirement inflation.

26. B
Unless the house was bought by Mrs. Simpson with money earned prior to marriage, or with gift or inheritance money, the house is community property. The question does not provide this information, and it cannot be assumed. Therefore, Mrs. Simpson's half of the house will pass by will. Mr. Simpson already owns half of the house under community property laws.

27. D

A second-to-die whole life policy is typically purchased for estate liquidity or to fund a specific goal at the death of the second spouse. Neither of these objectives are stated in the question. With the universal life policy, Stephen would not be forced to pay the annual premium. The question states that Stephen would like to purchase a policy that forces him to save money. A whole life policy will force Stephen to pay premiums, act as a forced savings plan, and last for his entire lifetime.

28. B

Buying a call and selling a put are bullish strategies. Investors choose these options when they expect the stock market to rise. Buying a put and selling a call are bearish strategies. Investors choose these options when they expect the stock market to decline in value.

29. B

Investment interest expense calculation:
Step 1: Identify the investment income: $9,000
Step 2: $4,000 (fees) - $2,400 (2% of AGI) = $1,600
Step 3: $9,000 - $1,600 = $7,400

30. B

In a complex trust, income may be distributed, but it is not required. The trustee has the discretion to accumulate income. A simple trust must distribute all of its income annually.

31. C

For a profit sharing plan, contributions may be skewed to favor older participants through methods such as age-weighting and cross-testing. Therefore, contributions do not need to be allocated on a pro-rata basis. The allocation formula cannot be discriminatory. Although profit sharing contributions must be substantial and recurring, the allocation formula must still be definite and predetermined.

32. C

Crummey powers provide a right of withdrawal equal to the lesser of the amount of the annual exclusion or the value of the gift transferred. In this question, the value of the gift exceeds the annual exclusion, so the withdrawal right is limited to $13,000.

33. C

A defined benefit plan is subject to the ERISA requirements for qualified plans, including participation, funding, and vesting. ERISA also imposes certain reporting and disclosure requirements. This information is disclosed to plan participants and filed with the IRS. A defined benefit plan is required to have insurance provided by the PBGC.

34. A

n = 15 x 12 = 180
i = 6.5/12 = 0.5417
PV = -$150,000
FV = 0
PMT = ? = $1,306.66
$1,306.66 x 180 = $235,199
$235,199 - $150,000 (principal) = $85,199

35. A

Mark can retire at age 63½ and receive COBRA coverage for 18 months. The question states that Mark works for a large company, so it can be assumed the company has twenty or more employees. At age 65, Mark will be eligible for Medicare.

36. D

ADRs allow for the trading of international securities in domestic countries. They trade throughout the day, and their dividends are declared in local currencies and paid in US dollars. ADR holders receive foreign tax credits for income tax paid to a foreign country.

37. B

The S&P index has systematic risk only. Systematic risk is also referred to as non-diversifiable risk. The other answers (non-systematic risk, diversifiable risk, and unsystematic risk) all refer to the same type of risk.

38. C

Dr. Lyons can avoid probate by titling his property as JTWROS, placing it in a revocable living trust, or placing it in an irrevocable trust. The revocable living trust and irrevocable trust would accomplish the same objective because the revocable trust becomes irrevocable at death and avoids probate. If Dr. Lyons delivered the deed to an escrow agent, that is considered a completed gift and avoids probate. The testamentary trust would not avoid probate because it is created by the will. Therefore, any property passing through the testamentary trust must first pass through probate.

39. D

Susan's personal use of the beach house can be the longer of 14 days, or 10% of the rental period. The rental period is 150 days (5 months x 30 days), so Susan can personally use the beach house for 15 days.

40. A

The required annual payment is the lesser of 90% of the current year's estimated tax bill, or 100% of last year's tax bill. If last year's tax return reported income over $150,000, Mary would have pay 110%, instead of 100%. The question states that Mary expects her current year tax liability to be $24,000. She can pay 90% of $24,000, equal to $21,600.

41.A
Any income retained by a PSC is taxed at a flat 35% rate, instead of the graduated corporate tax rates. The S Corp and LLC are pass-through entities which are not subject to graduated corporate tax rates. Only the C Corp is subject to graduated corporate tax rates.

42. C
Restricted stock is typically subject to forfeiture for the misconduct or termination of an executive. The other compensation plans listed are less likely to have such restrictions. Instead, they allow the executive to exercise the options within a specified period of time.

43. D
A stock with a beta of -1.5 will move 150% in the opposite direction of the market. If the stock market increases by 8%, the stock will decrease by 12% (8% x -1.5 = -12%).

44. C
C is the answer by process of elimination. Start with the securities with a beta of 1.1 and select the one of the highest return. This eliminates security B. Next, compare the securities that have an investment return of 10% and choose the one with the least risk (lowest beta). This eliminates security D. Finally, compare the two securities that are left, A and C. Security C gives you a higher return for less risk than security A. Therefore, security C is the investment a rational investor would choose.

45. D
The main objective of a prenuptial agreement is to address the accumulated assets each party brings to the marriage.

46.A
Jack has given his grandchildren a remainder interest in the condo. He did not give a reversionary interest because the condo does not return to Jack. A term interest would be for a limited time only, but the question states "for the rest of his life". A life estate would give Jack a controlling interest for his life, which he does not have.

47. C
In a limited partnership, the general partner has unlimited liability. A sole proprietorship does not provide liability protection. The LLC, C Corp, and S Corp will protect investors from liability beyond the amount they personally invested.

48. D
If the securities in a portfolio are perfectly correlated, then the standard deviation of the portfolio will be equal to the weighted average of the standard deviations of the individual securities within the portfolio. If the securities in a portfolio are not perfectly correlated, then the standard deviation of the portfolio will be less than the weighted average of the standard deviations of the individual securities making up the portfolio. By adding more securities to a portfolio, the standard deviation of the portfolio can never increase.

49. C
Subrogation refers to an insurance company's right to seek reimbursement from the person or entity legally responsible for an accident after the insurer has paid money to the insured.

50. C
Other-than-collision coverage will pay for losses that result from flood, vandalism, falling objects, and impact with an animal. Impact with a tree is considered collision.

51. B
There is an inverse relationship between interest rates, coupon payments, and duration. As interest rates and coupon payments decrease, duration increases. There is a direct relationship between time to maturity and duration. The longer the time to maturity, the longer the duration. A bond's quality does not directly impact its duration.

52. B
Form 706 is for the federal estate tax return. Form 709 is for the gift tax and GSTT. It may be helpful to remember that form 706 is filed when the decedent is "6 feet under".

53. B
With a CRUT, the 6% payout would be paid based on the value of the trust assets revalued annually. Therefore, a payout of 6% based on the initial gift amount cannot be guaranteed.

54. C
Paying the payor spouse's mortgage does not qualify as alimony because Rita's ex-husband (the payor) owns the home. If Rita owned the home and her ex-husband paid the mortgage, then it would qualify as alimony. Child support payments are not considered alimony.

55. B
A target benefit plan is similar to a defined benefit plan because contributions are based on projected retirement benefits.

56. F
Defined contribution plans can be either pension plans or profit sharing plans.

57. E
A cash balance plan is a type of defined benefit plan that defines the employee's benefit in terms that are more characteristic of a defined contribution plan.

58. G
In a unit benefit plan, the employer calculates the contribution by multiplying an employee's years of service by a percentage of his or her salary.

59. A
A money purchase plan requires that a fixed percentage of compensation be contributed for each eligible employee.

60. B
Air travel provided to an airline employee is considered a no-additional-cost service. These services are tax-free.

61. B
Membership dues to business-related associations are considered a working condition fringe benefit. These benefits are tax-free.

62. A
The personal use of employer-provided lodging is a taxable non-cash fringe benefit.

63. A
Personal use of a corporate jet is a taxable non-cash fringe benefit.

64. A
The allowable discount for services is limited to 20% of the price at which the employer offers services to non-employees. The question states the employer provides a 30% discount.

65. A
If corporate bonds are selling at a significant premium, then newly issued bonds are selling with lower coupons. The corporations are likely to call their bonds and replace them with lower coupon bonds.

66. C
The widow and dependents of a covered employee are eligible for 36 months of COBRA coverage. There is no age restriction with COBRA. However, the child must be a dependent.

67. D

The employer can make your client wait until he has completed his second year of service to enroll in the plan. However, your client must become 100% immediately vested in all future contributions allocated to his account.

68. A

If Bert uses Ernie's property as a rental property, then Bert can do a like-kind exchange. Bert is not disqualified from doing a like-kind exchange simply because Ernie uses his property for non-business purposes. Ernie cannot do a like-kind exchange because he currently owns a home, not a rental property.

69. C

A CRAT can pay Professor Radford a fixed percentage of the initial FMV of the trust. With a CRUT, the annual payout would be based on the FMV of the trust corpus revalued annually.

70. A

There are seven principles and you need to know them in the correct order. The seven principles form the acronym "IOCFCPD". Ideas Only Come From Careful Planning Daily. Option A is the only answer that lists the principles in their correct order.

71. G

A salary reduction plan uses some portion of the employee's current compensation to fund the ultimate benefit.

72. B

A supplemental executive retirement plan (SERP) provides a retirement benefit in excess of the company's qualified plan benefit, and without regard to the IRC Section 415 limits.

73. A

An excess benefit plan provides the retirement benefit that would be paid under the company's qualified plan formula if the IRC Section 415 limits did not apply.

74. C

An unfunded deferred compensation plan provides the executive only with a promise to pay benefits at retirement.

75. B

There is no indication the client needs life insurance, and she will not be eligible to purchase disability insurance when she retires. Because the client is only 58 years old, she will need health insurance until she is eligible for Medicare at age 65. Even if she had COBRA coverage, it would not last until age 65. Long-term care insurance is the best remaining answer of the choices provided.

76. A
Securities Act of 1933: Regulates new securities
Securities Act of 1934: Regulates existing securities
Investment Company Act of 1940: Regulates mutual funds
SIPC of 1970: Regulates brokerage firms

77. D
An employee who contributes to a 457 plan is not considered an active participant for IRA contribution purposes.

78. B
Unpaid interest from an annuity is considered to be Income in Respect of a Decedent. Annuities bypass probate and pay proceeds to a named beneficiary.

79. B
HO-4 is a renter's policy that provides no coverage on the dwelling. It provides liability coverage and broad form coverage on personal property.

80. D
Interest rate risk is the risk that, as interest rates rise, bond prices will fall. Interest rate risk is measured by a bond's duration.

81. C
Taking more or less risk will move the investor's position along the efficient frontier, but will not shift it. The same is true of changing the proportion of securities already invested in the portfolio. However, by selecting investments with lower coefficients of correlation, the risk will be reduced and the efficient frontier will shift upward and to the left.

82. B
Evan's overall charitable deduction is limited to 50% of his AGI, or $75,000. Since the stock was held for less than one year, Evan's deduction is limited to the basis of $80,000. However, the 50% limit always applies, so only $75,000 can be deducted this year. The excess $5,000 is carried forward to next year.

83. D
All employees, age 21 or older, who performed services during the current year and earned at least $500 in three out of the past five years, must be eligible to participate in a SEP. Employer contributions to a SEP are not subject to FICA/FUTA withholding. A SEP does not need to provide for QPSA/QJSA. Loans are not permitted in any type of IRA.

84. D

For the 15% capital gains rate to apply, Miriam must be in a marginal tax bracket of 25% or higher. To qualify for long-term capital gains, assets must be held for more than one year.

85. D

Residual benefits cover partial disability and address your client's concern. The cost-of-living adjustment, waiver of premium, and change-of-occupation provision are valid, but do not address your client's concern.

86. A

Group survivors' income insurance is payable only to an employee's surviving spouse and children. No other beneficiary may be designated.

87. D

Group paid-up life insurance is a combination of two basic plans: accumulating units of permanent life insurance and decreasing units of group term life insurance.

88. E

Dependents' group life insurance must cover all eligible dependents if the employer pays the entire premium.

89. C

Group term life insurance pays a death benefit to the employee's named beneficiary if the employee dies while covered under the policy. A medical exam is usually not required.

90. C

Thirty continuing education (CE) hours are required per two year reporting period. However, during the first reporting period the required number of CE hours may be less than 30 depending on the CFP® practitioner's date of birth.

91. G

According to the assignment of income doctrine, income is taxed to the tree that grows the fruit, even though it may be assigned to another person prior to receipt.

92. D

Assigning a life insurance policy as security for a loan is an example of an assignment of interest.

93. F

A sham transaction lacks a business purpose and economic substance, and will be ignored for tax purposes.

94. E
The doctrine of constructive receipt is used to determine whether a taxpayer has received income. Unlike actual receipt, constructive receipt does not require physical possession.

95. C
According to the step transaction doctrine, individual transactions should be ignored and the ultimate transaction should be taxed instead.

96. A
A child, under age 18, who is employed by a parent in an unincorporated business, does not have to pay social security taxes.

97. B
Investors buy calls when they expect the stock market to rise. Investors buy puts and write calls when they expect the stock market to decline in value.

98. B
Ademption is the failure of a gift of property to be distributed according to the provisions of a will because the property no longer belongs to the testator at the time of death.

99. B
Michael's 60-day window to elect COBRA coverage begins after he receives notification from the plan administrator.

100. D
Tenancy by entirety is a form of joint tenancy allowed for married couples. It is severable only by both spouses, and the property automatically passes to the surviving spouse when the first spouse dies.

101. A
A portfolio with a beta of 1.0 will move in the exact direction as the overall stock market. Therefore, the portfolio has only market risk, also known as systematic risk.

102. A
Forfeitures from a pension plan can be reallocated to remaining participants or used to decrease employer contributions. The question states that forfeitures are not reallocated to remaining participants, so they must be used to decrease employer contributions.

103. A
It is assumed the recent college graduate will have a lower starting salary than the highly compensated employee. This will decrease employer contributions.

104. A
Lower salary levels for all employees will decrease employer contributions.

105. C
Investment returns do not effect employer contributions in a pension plan. The employee assumes the investment risk.

106. C
A change in interest rate has the most significant impact on a low coupon bond.

107. B
In a revocable living trust, income is passed through to the individual who will pay it personally. The trust itself is tax-neutral.

108. C
The permitted disparity is the lesser of the base percentage (22.50%), or 26.25%. The excess percentage is 22.50% + 22.50% = 45.00%.

109. B
If Mr. Smith becomes disabled, his stock will be redeemed for $1,000,000, producing a gain of $800,000. At Mr. Smith's death, his estate will receive a step-up in basis and no tax will be due on the life insurance proceeds.

110. B
(9.0% - 4.5%) x 0.8 = 3.6%. The stock risk premium is the part of the CAPM equation located inside the parenthesis, multiplied by the stock's beta.

111. C
A deduction is more beneficial to a high-bracket taxpayer, and a credit is more beneficial to a low-bracket taxpayer.

112. D
When gift splitting is elected, all gifts must be split for that particular year.

113. A
Selling a stock short without already owning the stock would put an investor at the greatest risk. If the stock increases in value, the investor would have to repurchase the stock on the open market. However, if the investor already owned the stock, she would benefit from the shares appreciating in value.

114. B
The tax clause, debts clause, and residuary clause will likely affect how much Claire will receive from Paul's will.

115. D
Blue chip common stocks provide a hedge against inflation. Growth stocks typically reinvest their earnings back into the company rather than pay dividends to shareholders. GNMA securities, not FNMA, are backed by the US government. Global funds invest in both US and international companies.

116. B
If zero-coupon bonds were held in a taxable account, tax would be due on the interest earned each year, even though no interest was paid out. However, in an IRA, the interest would be tax deferred.

117. C
Treasury regulations are considered the most authoritative, and would carry the highest precedential value in defending a client's tax position against the IRS.

118. B
Participating life insurance policies pay dividends; non-participating policies do not.

119. A
Only defined benefit plans are subject to the PBGC. The only defined benefit plan listed is the cash balance plan.

120. C
The investor's best choice is to buy a put. When an investor expects a large increase or decrease in a stock's price, she should buy a call or put, respectively. If the investor expects only a small change in value, and is mainly interested in premium income, she should sell a call or put. In this question, selling a call may be a valid strategy, but the best answer is to buy a put.

121. D
A home can be rented for up to 14 days per year without any tax consequences.

122. B
Because she will reach age 70½ in the same year she turns 71, she must use age 71 when calculating her first distribution.

123. B
The elements of an insurable risk are:
1. The loss must be due to chance.
2. There must be a large number of homogeneous exposure units to make losses reasonably predictable.
3. The loss must be definite and measurable.
4. The loss cannot be catastrophic.

124. A
Kurtosis refers to the thickness of the tail on a normal distribution chart of investment returns. A thin tail (low kurtosis) means investments returns are bunched towards the mean. A risk-averse investor prefers low kurtosis.

High kurtosis = fat tail
Low kurtosis = thin tail

125. A
A QDOT allows property to pass to a non-US citizen spouse and still qualify for the marital deduction. In order for a QDOT to be valid, there must be at least one trustee who is a US citizen or a qualifying domestic corporation.

126. C
Susan's stock receives a full step-up in basis at her death. Lifetime gifts do not receive a step-up in basis.

127. B
Corporate investors in preferred stock can generally deduct 70% of the dividends they receive.

128. D
Cash donations to qualified public charities are limited to 50% of the taxpayer's adjusted gross income. The excess amount is carried forward. For Steve, 50% of his AGI last year was $37,500. Therefore, last year, Steve could only deduct $37,500 of the $40,000 gift. The remaining $2,500 is carried forward to this year, when it can be deducted by Steve.

129. D
Regardless of income, participating in a 457 plan does not affect the deductibility of Marie's IRA contribution. Participating in a 401k or 403b would eliminate Marie's ability to deduct her IRA contribution because her income is over the threshold.

130. D
A 403b plan may be adopted by an employer that is a state, agency of a state, nonprofit organization, public university, or private university.

131. C
A single life annuity will provide the maximum payout to Jessica. A single life annuity is also referred to as a "pure life" annuity.

132. D
Ryan will owe individual income tax plus self-employment tax (social security and Medicare) on his independent contractor income.

133. D
Future dividends may not be guaranteed at all. Many mutual life insurance companies issue participating policies.

134. C
Variable life insurance policies have fixed premiums and provide a guaranteed minimum death benefit. The cash value is linked to the performance of the underlying investments, which may include the S&P 500.

135. D
The conversion provision in a life insurance policy allows an insured to convert from term insurance to permanent insurance without having to show evidence of insurability.

136. C
Stanley is registered through his firm, so he is only a person associated with an investment adviser. Stanley must disclose his firm's status as a registered investment adviser.

137. A
A MEC is a life insurance contract that fails to meet the "seven-pay test".

138. B
Section 303 provides for redemption of corporate stock to be treated as a sale, rather than a dividend. Section 6166 allows for the deferral of estate taxes, but does not reduce taxes. Section 2503(c) allows for an annual exclusion from a trust that is set up for a minor. Section 2032(a) allows for special use valuation for real estate, not corporate stock.

139. A
A Rabbi trust is a revocable trust, but it may become irrevocable if there is a change in corporate control. The trust may not include a bankruptcy trigger because corporate executives could obtain benefits before creditors. The corporation may contribute general corporate assets to the trust if the assets remain subject to the corporation's general creditors.

140. B
An employer's annual contributions to a defined benefit plan will increase when the investment returns are lower than expected. A high ratio of married to unmarried participants will also increase employer contributions because pre-retirement death benefits are required for married participants, but not for unmarried participants. High turnover will reduce employer contributions, especially if it leads to large forfeitures. Large forfeitures will provide more funds to pay benefits, resulting in less employer contributions.

141. C
A life insurance policy's cash value can be used to provide collateral for a loan, or as an asset to help grow a business. The difference between a policy's face amount and the reserve may be more than, less than, or equal to the cash surrender value at different points in a policy's life. However, the reserve must equal the face amount by the end of the mortality table. Premiums do not have to be paid for an insured's entire lifetime, and there is not a ten-year minimum.

142. C
Stock market anomalies should not occur if markets are fully efficient. They do not support the efficient market hypothesis.

143. D
In a private annuity, no future payments are due to the seller or her estate at death. Therefore, a private annuity is not included in the decedent's gross estate.

144. A
Open-end mutual funds sell at their net asset value and issue new stock whenever an individual buys shares. Closed-end mutual funds may sell for a price that is greater than their net asset value (premium), or less than their net asset value (discount). With only a certain number of shares available, closed-end mutual funds have a fixed capital structure.

145. D
IRAs may invest in all four types of investments, including real estate (REITs).

146. B

Stephanie's call option is out-of-the-money because the strike price ($22.00) exceeds the market price ($21.50). An option cannot have a negative intrinsic value. Therefore, the value of the option is $0.

147. D

An antique is a collectible, and IRAs are not permitted to invest in collectibles. John's purchase will be treated as a distribution from his IRA equal to the cost of the antique in the year of purchase.

148. B

Covered care may be provided in a variety of settings, and Medicare does not provide sufficient coverage because of various limitations and restrictions. Long-term care coverage must be provided for at least twelve months.

149. D

The beta coefficient is calculated by dividing the standard deviation of the return for a security by the standard deviation of the return for the overall market, and then multiplying the result by the correlation coefficient of the two returns. Refer to the formula sheet.

150. B

The applicable credit amount changes according to a schedule set by Congress. It is not adjusted for inflation.

151. C

Mike is permitted to deduct losses up to his basis of $65,000. The money Mike lent the company ($20,000) is added to his initial investment ($40,000) to total $65,000.

152. A

A CRAT provides fixed income that is a sum certain.

153. D

Both a CRAT and CRUT can provide income to the grantor for life, along with a deduction for the charitable contribution of the remainder interest.

154. C

Neither CRATs nor CRUTs provide immediate income to charity. Instead, they provide an interest to charity after income has been paid to the grantor. A charitable lead trust (CLT) provides immediate income to charity.

155. B
A CRUT provides variable income because the income is based on the value of the trust assets revalued annually.

156. A
To determine the loss on the sale of a gift, the donee's basis is the lower of the donor's basis or the FMV of the property when the donee receives it. Although Rob's basis was $8,000, the value of the gift when Bill received it was only $3,000, which becomes his new basis. Therefore, Bill realized a $1,000 loss when he sold the sculpture for $2,000.

157. C
Dr. Krier can deduct his home office expenses only if he uses the office exclusively for business activities. It must be either his principal place of business, or where he meets with patients in the normal course of business. The home office deduction cannot generate a loss to be used against income from Dr. Krier's other activities.

158. B
Profit sharing plans tend to favor younger employees, and they are not limited in their investment of company stock. Profit sharing plans are a type of defined contribution plan other than a pension plan. Their contributions must be substantial and recurring, but are not required annually.

159. B
Alimony is taxable to the payee and deductible by the payor. Premiums paid on up to $50,000 of group term life insurance are not considered taxable income to an employee. However, the question states that coverage is for $100,000. Therefore, a portion will be taxable. Child support payments and workers compensation are not taxable income.

160. C
The value of publicly traded stocks and bonds is the mean between the highest and lowest quoted selling price on the date of disposition for gift and estate tax purposes.

161. B
The trust will be a grantor trust, and income will be taxed to Brian if he retains the right to control the beneficial enjoyment of the trust. If Brian adds his nephew as a beneficiary, he will be changing the beneficial enjoyment. Some exceptions to this rule are for the powers to sprinkle or accumulate income. Another exception is the power to invade the trust principal for a beneficiary's health, education, maintenance, and support (HEMS).

162. D
All the interests listed may be disclaimed by filing a qualified disclaimer.

163. A
Money purchase plans are easy to explain to employees because contributions are based on a flat percentage of compensation. Money purchase plans tend to favor younger employees, and forfeitures can be reallocated to remaining employees. Contributions cannot be omitted in bad years. The "substantial and recurring" rule only applies to profit sharing plans.

164. A
A payment made to a third party will qualify as alimony if it's made to satisfy an obligation to the spouse. This applies whether it's required pursuant to a written separation agreement or a divorce decree. A transfer of investment property does not qualify as alimony because alimony must be paid in cash. A fixed payment that is discontinued upon the occurrence of an event related to a child is treated as child support.

165. C
The bargain element of ISOs, and the difference between accelerated depreciation and straight line depreciation are subject to AMT. Interest on private purpose municipal bonds is an adjustment for AMT, but interest on general obligation municipal bonds is not.

166. D
Both a special and a general power of appointment give the holder the ability to appoint funds held by another entity.

167. B
Assets subject to a general power of appointment are includible in the holder's gross estate at death.

168. A
A power that can be exercised only with the consent of an adverse party is considered a special power of appointment.

169. B
A holder's release of a general power of appointment results in a gift for federal gift tax purposes.

170. D
A fixed income security may be subject to all the risks listed. This includes systematic risks that are always present (exchange rate risk, purchasing power risk, reinvestment rate risk), as well as non-systematic risks such as default risk and liquidity risk.

171. B
Wills do not avoid probate. Planning for incapacity is addressed through powers of attorney, not through the will. The will is often read after the decedent's funeral, so burial wishes should not be included in the will.

172. B
A living will is a legal document in which an individual specifies what type of medical treatment she prefers in the event of an emergency. Specifically, it addresses the individual's wishes about artificial life support. A living will is also known as an advance medical directive.

173. A
Alimony payments, government loans, and child support payments are not dischargeable through bankruptcy.

174. A
A first-time home purchase and qualified education costs are among the exemptions from the 10% early withdrawal penalty. Hardship withdrawals, and withdrawals made after separating from service at age 55 or older are permitted in 401k plans but not IRAs. Loans from IRAs are not allowed.

175. A
The non-forfeiture options are paid-up reduced amount, cash, and extended term.

176. B
Johnny's income is earned, so the kiddie tax rules don't apply. A child, under age 18, who is employed by a parent in an unincorporated business, does not have to pay social security taxes.

177. B
A PSC cannot pass earnings or losses through to its shareholders. Any income retained by a PSC is taxed at a flat 35% rate, instead of the graduated corporate tax rates. Both S Corps and PSCs provide a step-up in basis at death, limited liability, and deductions for business expenses.

178. D
The intrinsic value of an option can never be negative. The LMN option is out-of-the money ($0), and the XYZ option is in-the-money and has a value of $3.

179. A
Business equipment is eligible for a like-kind exchange. Securities and inventory are not eligible. Livestock of different sexes do not qualify for a like-kind exchange, but same sex livestock will qualify.

180. B
Amos will get 80% of his full primary insurance amount (PIA), equal to a 20% reduction. The reduction is equal to 5/9 of 1% for each month social security is taken early.

The social security reduction is calculated as follows:
5/9 = 0.5556
0.5556 x .01 = 0.005556
0.005556 x 36 = 0.20

181. B
Defined benefit plans and target benefit plans are required to use actuarial calculations. Defined benefit plans require annual actuarial calculations. Target benefit plans require an actuarial calculation only at the inception of the plan.

182. B
By selling a naked call, Chris is expecting Google's stock price to decrease. If Google stock increases in value, Chris' potential loss is unlimited.

183. B
The participant's retirement benefit in a defined contribution plan is based on the account balance. The account balance is affected by the investment performance. Pre-retirement inflation will likely affect salary levels and, therefore, affect the contribution amount. The participant's life expectancy does not directly affect the account balance in a defined contribution plan.

184. D
The purchase date (January 20) is within thirty days of the sale date (December 30), and would be considered a wash sale. This means the loss deduction is disallowed. The amount of the disallowed loss will be added to the cost basis of the shares Joel purchased on January 20.

185. C
This is a bargain sale to charity. The taxable gain is calculated as follows:
Step 1: $400,000 (sale price) / $800,000 (FMV) = 50%
Step 2: 50% x $200,000 (basis) = $100,000
Step 3: $400,000 (sale price) - $100,000 = $300,000 taxable gain

186. B
Individual account balances are unknown in defined benefit plans. They are only known in defined contribution plans, such as target benefit plans. Contributions are determined through actuarial assumptions for both target benefit plans and defined benefit plans.

187. C
The Sterns should first estimate their income and sources of income. Next, they should review their fixed and discretionary expenses before determining how much will be saved or invested.

188. C
The 529 plan and PLUS loan are not based on financial need. The Perkins loan and subsidized Stafford student loan are highly based on financial need, and Grady and Donna's child will likely not qualify.

189. A
Indemnity is protection from liabilities or penalties incurred by one's actions. It is enforced through the principle of subrogation. Subrogation refers to an insurance company's right to seek reimbursement from the person or entity legally responsible for an accident after the insurer has paid money to the insured.

190. B
The defined benefit plan would provide the greatest benefit to Ryan because he has five younger employees, and defined benefit plans favor older owner/employees. Of the other options listed, the age-based profit sharing plan is a valid consideration. However, the question says to assume adequate cash flow in the business. Profit sharing plans would benefit unstable cash flow because contributions must only be substantial and recurring. The best answer is the defined benefit plan.

191. D
Gambling losses to the extent of winnings are not subject to the 2% of AGI floor. Deductions subject to the 2% of AGI floor include professional and business association dues, the costs of looking for a new job, and work uniforms not suitable for regular wear.

192. C
JTWROS, Totten trusts, tenancy by entirety, and payable on death accounts avoid probate. Tenancy in common and community property are subject to probate.

193. B
All of the sources of income listed are includible in determining the taxation of Charlie's social security benefits, except worker's compensation.

194. B
Failure to pay: 0.5% of the tax due per month, up to a maximum of 25%
Failure to file: 5% of the tax due per month, up to a maximum of 25%
Negligence: 20% of the underpayment attributed to negligence

Civil fraud: 75% of the underpayment attributed to civil fraud
Tax return preparer understates the amount of tax owed: $1,000 penalty

195. D

Only the cost for up to $50,000 of group term life insurance coverage is excludible from an employee's income. However, an employer can deduct its contribution to a group term life insurance plan regardless of the amount of coverage it provides.

196. C

When ISOs are exercised, the bargain element is an AMT preference item but there is no AMT withholding. ISOs are not subject to FICA withholding at the time of exercise.

197. D

In an unfunded deferred compensation plan, all payments are taxed as ordinary income when received and subject to social security taxes.

198. A

Pete will recognize $3,000 of ordinary income at retirement. The remaining $12,000 will be taxed as capital gains.

199. D

When property is transferred for less than full consideration of money or money's worth, the value of the gift is equal to the value of the property transferred less the consideration received. Only the value of transferred property with no offsetting consideration is ruled a gift for tax purposes.

200. D

Withdrawals from a 401k after separating from service are penalty-free if the separation occurs at age 55 or older. The other options would result in an early withdrawal penalty.

201. C

The home owned as community property, the insurance policy owned by the decedent, and the IRA without a named beneficiary are all included in the probate estate. The other items would be included in the decedent's gross estate, but not the probate estate.

202. C

Preferred stock does not have a fixed maturity date. Therefore, it has unlimited interest rate risk.

203. C
Money market funds can be redeemed at any time without penalty. Their objective is to earn interest for shareholders.

204. E
A certificate of deposit is intended to be held until maturity, but can be redeemed prior to maturity for a penalty.

205. D
Commercial paper is an unsecured promissory note issued by a corporation with a fixed maturity of up to 270 days.

206. B
Treasury bonds pay a fixed rate of interest every six months until maturity. They are issued in terms of ten years or more.

207. F
American Depository Receipt dividends are declared in local currencies and paid in US dollars.

208. B
International mutual funds invest in the equity securities of companies located outside the US. Global mutual funds invest in both international and domestic companies.

209. C
Universal life insurance policies have a flexible premium and death benefit. They are said to have an "unbundled structure". Universal life policies do not have a minimum guaranteed cash value.

210. C
Determining the duration of the engagement is part of the first step of the financial planning process: Establishing and defining the client-planner relationship.

211. A
Interviewing the client and using a fact-finding questionnaire is part of the second step of the financial planning process: Gathering client data, including goals.

212. E
Determining the client's financial status is part of the third step of the financial planning process: Analyzing and evaluating the client's financial status.

213. D
Selecting suitable strategies for goal achievement and recommending to the client is part of the fourth step of the financial planning process: Developing and presenting recommendations and/or alternatives.

214. B
Assisting the client as needed to carry out the recommended plan is part of the fifth step of the financial planning process: Implementing the financial planning recommendations.

215. F
Reviewing changes in the client's circumstances and evaluating the performance of the plan is part of the sixth step of the financial planning process: Monitoring the financial plan.

216. A
Stock dividends are distributions by a corporation that are paid as additional shares of stock rather than cash.

217. D
A qualified dividend is a type of dividend to which capital gain tax rates are applied.

218. E
A disguised dividend, such as a below-market shareholder loan, is considered to be a constructive dividend.

219. F
A payment to shareholders that exceeds the company's retained earnings is a liquidating dividend. The payment is made from capital rather than earnings.

220. G
Stock rights allow an investor to subscribe to additional shares of stock at a set price.

221. B
The family limited partnership and QPRT can reduce your client's gross estate. The Totten trust and living trust will reduce the probate estate, but not the gross estate.

222. C
A QPRT is commonly used for vacation homes, and homes valued over $1,000,000. The grantor will have a taxable gift upon the creation of a QPRT.

223. B
By dividing 72 by the annual interest rate, an investor can determine how many years it will take for her initial investment to double.

72/6 = 12 years

224. D
An intentional tort is a civil wrong resulting from an intentional act. An unintentional tort results from negligence or carelessness, and there is no intention to cause harm.

225. D
Neither ISOs nor NSOs are taxed at the time of grant. The tax treatment is different between ISOs and NSOs at the time of exercise and at the time of sale.

Part 4:

CASE STUDIES

CASE STRATEGY

The following five-step process will help you complete the cases with more accuracy and less frustration. In total, the cases make up about sixty questions, or 20 percent of the exam. Without successfully completing the cases, you'll have a difficult time passing. Read the following steps and apply them to the case that follows. Analysis and supporting documents are also provided.

Step 1: Skim the questions to see if there's an emphasis on any particular topics. Shorter cases will often emphasize a few specific topics. By identifying these topics early, you'll know where to better focus your reading.
<1 minute

Step 2: Quickly read the case. The goal of this step is to identify the names, ages, and dates listed in the case. Highlight all of these, even if they appear in the footnotes. This information will be useful later. Also highlight any numbers that are spelled out. By focusing on names, ages, and dates, you'll be able to quickly get a feel for the case without wasting valuable time reading too carefully.
<3 minutes

Step 3: Make your first pass through the questions by answering those you know, and circling those you don't. Use your knowledge of the case to identify where each answer is likely to be found. Find that section, and spend a few seconds trying to locate the answer. If you can't find the answer quickly, circle it and move on.
<10 minutes

Step 4: Once you've attempted all the case questions one time, go back to the questions you circled and try answering them. Now that you've read all the questions at least once, you may have picked up an extra detail that will help you determine the right answer.
<5 minutes

Step 5: If there are still questions you can't answer, eliminate the choices you know are incorrect, and take your best guess.
<1 minute

Total time per case: 20 minutes

BONSELL CASE

Use the following information about Mike and Renee Bonsell to answer questions 1 through 15.

MIKE AND RENEE BONSELL

The Bonsells have come to you for assistance in developing their financial plan. From your initial meeting, you've gathered the following information.

PERSONAL DATA

- Married 35 years
- Two children: Garrett, age 33, and Jane, age 29
- Garrett is married with three children, ages 6, 5, and 2
- Jane is divorced and has two children, ages 5 and 3

Mike Bonsell

- Age 59
- Chief Financial Officer for a publishing company
- Freelance writer

Renee Bonsell

- Age 57
- Floral designer

INSURANCE INFORMATION

- Mike and Renee have liability limits of $50,000/$100,000/$25,000 on their autos. Their collision and other-than-collision deductibles are $100 each.
- They have an HO-3 policy on their home. Their coverage is as follows: $110,000 on the dwelling, $10,000 on other structures, $22,000 for loss of use, and $50,000 personal liability coverage.
- Group health insurance is provided through Mike's employer, covering both Mike and Renee. There is a $150 per year individual deductible, and a $300 per year family deductible. The coverage includes an 80% coinsurance clause, and a $2,000,000 maximum lifetime benefit.

- Mike's employer provides him with group term life insurance equal to four times his annual salary.

TAX INFORMATION

Income

- Mike's salary as Chief Financial Officer is $95,000 per year. He also earns $25,000 per year as a freelance writer.
- Renee's annual salary from the florist shop is $30,000.
- Mike and Renee do not anticipate an increase in their salary levels over the next few years.

Federal Income Tax

- The Bonsells are in the 28% federal income tax bracket.
- Mike and Renee file a joint tax return.

Property Tax

- $4,000 per year

INVESTMENT INFORMATION

- Money market fund: Yields 3.5% per year, which is reinvested into the fund.
- Savings account: Generates interest of $3,000 per year, which is withdrawn annually. The savings account is earmarked as the Bonsells' cash reserve.
- Value mutual fund: Purchased for $315,000. In the most recent year, the fund's return was -2%. In the previous three years, the investment returns were 5%, -1%, and 6%. All income is reinvested into the fund.
- Common stocks: Mike purchased six highly speculative bank stocks over twenty years ago for $24,500. The stocks are not currently paying a dividend. The expected return for the common stocks is 10%.
- 401k: Allocated 50% to a high-yield corporate bond fund and 50% to a conservative bond fund. The rate of return for the past five years has been 4%, 7%, 3%, 9%, and 6%. The expected return for the 401k is 5.5%.
- Age-weighted profit sharing plan: The profit sharing plan seeks a mix of income and long-term capital growth. The expected return is 6%. The contributions made by Renee's employer are expected to average $4,000 annually.
- Mike and Renee classify their risk tolerance level as moderate.

RETIREMENT INFORMATION

- Mike participates in his employer's 401k plan. He contributes the maximum allowable each year, and makes the full catch-up contribution. The publishing company matches 100% of the first 3% Mike contributes and 50% of the next 3%.
- Renee participates in her employer's age-weighted profit sharing plan. She's among the older employees at the florist shop, so she receives increased contributions and forfeitures compared to other employees.
- Mike and Renee each expect to receive social security benefits when Mike retires at his normal retirement age of 66. Mike's most recent social security statement estimates his benefit will be $19,500 per year when he retires.
- Mike and Renee expect to live twenty years beyond their retirement age.
- During retirement, Mike and Renee estimate their investment return will be 5.5% after tax.

ECONOMIC ENVIRONMENT

- Inflation is expected to average 3.5% per year both pre- and post-retirement.
- Mortgage interest rates are currently 5.50% for 30-year mortgages, and 4.75% for 15-year mortgages. The lender will require two points for settlement. If the Bonsells choose to refinance their home mortgage, they will pay the settlement points separately.

MIKE AND RENEE'S GOALS

1. The Bonsells would like to retire when Mike reaches age 66. After a thorough analysis of their current budget and projected retirement expenses, they determined their annual retirement need is $100,000 in today's dollars.

2. The Bonsells need to develop an estate plan. They currently have only outdated wills that haven't been reviewed since they were married thirty-five years ago. Mike and Renee would like to ensure that all assets will pass in equal amounts to their five grandchildren at death.

3. Mike would like to write and publish his own book after he retires, and Renee would like to volunteer at the local veterinary hospital. They do not expect to generate significant income after retirement.

Mike and Renee Bonsell
Statement of Financial Position
December 31, 20XX

ASSETS		LIABILITIES AND NET WORTH	
Cash/Cash Equivalents		**Liabilities**	
Checking account (H) [1]	$ 6,000	1st mortgage on home [3]	52,000
Savings account (H)	75,000	Home equity loan	17,700
Money market fund (W)	21,000	Credit card balance [4]	$ 21,000
		Car loans	19,400
Invested Assets			
Value mutual fund (JT)	$ 400,000	**TOTAL LIABILITIES**	$ 110,100
Common stocks (H)	295,000		
Retirement Assets			
401k (H)	$ 450,000		
Profit sharing plan (W)	35,000		
		NET WORTH	$1,436,900
Use Assets			
House (JT)	$ 175,000		
Personal property (JT) [2]	48,000		
Autos (JT)	42,000		
TOTAL ASSETS	$1,547,000		

1. H = Mike as owner, W = Renee as owner, JT = Joint tenants with right of survivorship
2. Includes jewelry valued at $15,000
3. 6.5%, 30-year fixed rate mortgage; principal amount last year was $56,200
4. 14.99% APR

Mike and Renee Bonsell
Cash Flow Statement
January 1, 20XX through December 31, 20XX

INFLOWS

Mike's salary	$ 95,000
Mike's freelance writing income	25,000
Renee's salary	30,000
Investment income	3,000
TOTAL INFLOWS	**$ 153,000**

OUTFLOWS

US Income and FICA taxes	$ 53,500
Contributions to 401k	22,000
Car loans	16,000
Credit cards	10,000
Mortgage	10,600
Food and supplies	6,000
Auto and homeowners insurance	5,000
Clothing	5,000
Home equity loan	4,400
Property taxes	4,000
Travel and entertainment	4,000
Charitable contributions	4,000
Medical and dental	3,000
Transportation (gas, oil, repairs)	2,500
Utilities and household expenses	2,000
Maintenance and repairs on home	1,000
TOTAL OUTFLOWS	**$ 153,000**

BONSELL CASE QUESTIONS

1. **What was the original amount of the first mortgage taken out by Mike and Renee Bonsell?**

   A. $101,500
   B. $139,752
   C. $158,220
   D. $181,565

2. **What is the standard deviation of the rates of return for the value mutual fund over the last four years?**

   A. 3
   B. 4
   C. 5
   D. 6

3. **Which of the following is the least suitable recommendation to the Bonsells in order to provide additional retirement savings?**

   A. Contribute to a SEP IRA for Mike
   B. Contribute to a Traditional IRA for Mike
   C. Contribute to a Roth IRA for Mike
   D. Contribute to a Roth IRA for Renee

4. **Do the Bonsells have a sufficient cash reserve? Assume they are comfortable having a cash reserve equal to three months of living expenses.**

   A. No, their money market fund is valued at $21,000, and three months of living expenses is $38,250.
   B. No, they should have six months of living expenses set aside as their cash reserve, and they are currently underfunding that goal.
   C. Yes, their savings account is valued at $75,000 and three months of living expenses is $38,250.
   D. Yes, they can withdraw money from Mike's 401k because he is over age 55 and has separated from service.

5. **What is the effective annual rate being charged on the credit card if the APR is calculated on a monthly basis?**

   A. 14.3%
   B. 16.1%
   C. 19.2%
   D. 21.4%

6. **How would you classify the overall portfolio of investments owned by Mike and Renee? Consider all of their investments, including retirement accounts.**

   A. A. Balanced
   B. B. Highly conservative
   C. C. Highly risky
   D. D. Focused on income production

7. **Which of the following concerns should be addressed first in the Bonsells' estate plan?**

   A. Special needs planning for the grandchildren
   B. Lack of burial wishes in the will
   C. Lack of updated wills and powers of attorney
   D. Lack of liquidity if Mike dies today

8. **Mike's employer is considering offering a split-dollar life insurance policy. All of the following statements concerning split-dollar life insurance are correct, except:**

   A. The plan may be offered by Mike's employer on a discriminatory basis.
   B. The employer contributes an amount equal to the annual increase in cash value.
   C. The corporation receives death benefits in an amount equal to the net amount at risk.
   D. Mike is permitted to select a beneficiary who will receive a portion of the death benefit.

9. **At the present rate of payment on the first mortgage, approximately how many additional months will be needed to fully pay off the debt?**

   A. 60 months
   B. 72 months
   C. 84 months
   D. 96 months

10. **What is the maximum amount that Renee can borrow from her profit sharing plan this year?**

    A. $10,000
    B. $17,500
    C. $35,000
    D. $50,000

11. **Mike and Renee are considering gifting their value mutual fund to their grandchildren to fund their college education. Which of the following is true regarding this potential gift?**

    A. The gift would be considered a direct skip for GSTT purposes and the grandchildren would be responsible for paying the tax.
    B. The gift would be considered a direct skip for GSTT purposes and Mike and Renee would be responsible for paying the tax.
    C. The gift would be considered a taxable distribution for GSTT purposes and the grandchildren would be responsible for paying the tax.
    D. The gift would be considered a taxable distribution for GSTT purposes and Mike and Renee would be responsible for paying the tax.

12. **All of the following are suitable recommendations for the Bonsells' insurance coverage, except:**

    A. Add an umbrella policy
    B. Add disability insurance for Renee
    C. Reduce the deductible on the auto policy
    D. Add long-term care insurance for both Mike and Renee

13. **Mike and Renee would like to buy a sailboat to use during the summer. They contacted their local bank and prequalified for a five-year loan. Under the terms of the loan, Mike and Renee would repay the bank by making a series of equal annual payments, beginning at the end of each of the next five years. The loan payments could be classified as which of the following?**

    A. A deferred annuity
    B. An annuity
    C. An annuity due
    D. A loan annuity

14. **If Mike and Renee each purchase a disability insurance policy, which definition of disability will be most favorable to them, and least desirable by the insurer?**

    A. Any occupation
    B. Own occupation
    C. Split definition
    D. No enough information is known

15. **If Mike dies this year, what will be the value of his gross estate for federal estate tax purposes?**

    A. $1,158,500
    B. $1,358,500
    C. $1,538,500
    D. $1,738,500

ANSWER SHEET

Question	Your Answer	Correct Answer	Notes
1			
2			
3			
4			
5			
6			
7			
8			
9			
10			
11			
12			
13			
14			
15			

NOTES:

BONSELL CASE ANALYSIS

Step 1:   After skimming the case questions, it seems like there's an even distribution of questions to topics. In a case with this many questions, you'll often see a comprehensive list of topics covered. I do not consider this an advantage, because there's no specific area to focus your attention.

Step 2:   Quickly reading the case and highlighting the names, ages, and dates takes about three minutes. In that short amount of time, you'll see the Bonsells are a family of four with two grown children. You'll learn that Mike and Renee are nearing retirement, and have assets valued over $1,500,000. It may not seem significant yet, but identifying names, ages, and dates has allowed you to absorb a lot of useful information that will save you time when you start answering questions.

Step 3:   Start working through the questions. If you're unsure of an answer, don't panic. There are multiple questions about each subject, so you may be able to narrow down your answers after reading the rest of the questions.

Step 4:   Your first time through the case you should have been able to answer at least ten questions. For those you couldn't answer, try once more, but don't waste too much time.

Step 5:   If you're still unsure about an answer, mark a letter and move on. This case should not take more than twenty minutes to complete.

BONSELL CASE ANSWERS

1. B
n = 30 x 12 = 360
i = 6.5/12 = 0.5417
PMT = $10,600/12= $883.33
FV = 0
PV = ? = $139,752

2. B
2, CHS, $\sum$
5, $\sum$
1, CHS, $\sum$
6, $\sum$
Blue g, s = 4.08248
Rounded to 4

3. B
Because Mike is an active participant in his publishing company's 401k, he will not be able to deduct contributions to a traditional IRA. Instead, Mike and Renee should contribute to a Roth IRA because their AGI is under the threshold. Mike can also contribute to a SEP IRA based on his freelance writing income.

4. C
According to the case, the Bonsells have earmarked their savings account as their cash reserve. The savings account has a balance of $75,000, which exceeds three months of living expenses.

5. B
n = 12
i = 14.99/12 = 1.24917
PV = -100
PMT = 0
FV = ? = 116.06
116.06 – 100 = 16.06
The answer is rounded to 16.1%.

6. A
Mike and Renee's investment portfolio can be described as "balanced" by process of elimination. The portfolio is not highly conservative because part of it is invested in speculative bank stocks and high-yield corporate bonds. It is not highly risky because part of the portfolio is invested in money market funds, a value mutual fund, and a con-

servative bond fund. The portfolio is not focused on income production because many of the Bonsells' investments produce little or no income.

7. C
Mike and Renee need to update their wills because they haven't been reviewed in thirty-five years. They also need to draft powers of attorney for health care, and financial powers of attorney. There is no indication that Mike and Renee's grandchildren have special needs, and burial wishes should not be included in the will.

8. C
In a split-dollar life insurance policy, the corporation receives a death benefit equal to the cash value, not the net amount at risk.

9. B
$i = 6.5/12 = 0.5417$
$PV = -\$52,000$
$PMT = \$10,600/12 = \$883.33$
$FV = 0$
$n = ? = 72$ months

10. B
Renee is permitted to borrow the lesser of $50,000 or one-half her account balance. Because her account balance is $35,000, Renee can borrow $17,500.

11. B
If Mike and Renee gift the value mutual fund to their grandchildren, the gift would be considered a direct skip for GSTT. Mike and Renee would be responsible for paying the tax.

12. C
Mike and Renee should consider purchasing umbrella insurance, disability insurance, and long-term care insurance. Their auto deductible is $100 and should not be adjusted lower.

13. B
A deferred annuity begins more than one period in the future. An annuity due requires payments to be made at the beginning of each period, not the end.

14. B
The "own occupation" definition of disability is most favorable to Mike and Renee because they will receive benefits if they become disabled and unable to perform the duties of their own occupation for which they were trained and educated.

15. C

$380,000	Group life insurance
$6,000	Checking
$75,000	Savings
$200,000	½ Value fund
$295,000	Common stock
$450,000	401k
$87,500	½ House
$24,000	½ Personal property
<u>$21,000</u>	½ Cars
$1,538,500	

CONCLUSION

You now have all the tools you need to successfully complete the CFP® Certification Exam. Preparing for the exam can easily become an overwhelming experience, but if you break down the process into the steps outlined in this guide, it will become much more manageable. There are no shortcuts, and your goal is to put yourself in the best possible position to pass the exam. This can only be achieved by following the recommended study schedule, maintaining a consistent pace, and accumulating three hundred hours of study time. Before you face the exam, make sure you've completed the following steps:

Step 1: Take the Diagnostic Practice Exam to see where you stand today and identify your weak areas. Scoring between 50 percent and 70 percent your first time through is average.

Step 2: Follow the recommended study schedule to raise your test scores to 80 percent or higher. Generally, an increase of 5 percent per month can be achieved if you follow the provided study schedule.

Step 3: Determine the date you'd like to take the exam based on the 5 percent per month rule. For example, if you're currently scoring 60 percent on practice tests, you'll need to study an additional four months to reach 80 percent.

Step 4: Use the blank worksheets provided in the Appendix to carefully track your progress.

Step 5: Reach a plateau by test day. If you continue scoring higher in the days immediately leading up to the exam, you may need additional study time. By the time you reach the exam, you should be reinforcing topics already learned, rather than learning new ones. Most test takers who successfully complete the exam reach a plateau between 80 percent and 85 percent by test day.

APPENDIX: BLANK WORKSHEETS

STUDY JOURNAL

Date	Hours of Study	Source	Unit	Notes

NOTES:

Date	Hours of Study	Source	Unit	Notes

NOTES:

STUDY JOURNAL – SAMPLE

Date	Hours of Study	Source	Unit	Notes
Tue 1/5	0.5	Keir Simulated Exam	All	Test #1
	0.5	Keir Simulated Exam	All	Test #1
	0.5	Keir Simulated Exam	All	Test #1
Wed 1/6	0.5	CFFP MC Workbook	Insurance	
	0.5	CFFP MC Workbook	Tax Planning	
	0.5	CFFP MC Workbook	Retirement	
	0.5	CFFP MC Workbook	Investments	
Thur 1/7	0.5	CFFP Practice Exam	All	Exam 1, Part 1
	0.5	CFFP Practice Exam	All	Exam 1, Part 1

PRACTICE TEST RESULTS

Date	Number of Times	Source	Correct	Attempted	% Correct
			Month 1:		
			Month 2:		
			Month 3:		
			Total:		

PRACTICE TEST RESULTS – SAMPLE

Date	Number of Times	Source	Correct	Attempted	% Correct
1/27 – 2/1	1	CFFP Practice Exam 1	204	285	71.6%
2/2 – 2/7	1	CFFP MC Workbook	467	609	76.7%
2/8	1	Keir MC Workbook	15	5	77.1%
2/9 – 2/11	2	CFFP Practice Exam 1	20	285	73.3%
2/12	1	Zah	68	82	82.9%
2/13		F r m	71	100	71.0%
2/14 – 2/17	1	Practice Exam 2	228	285	80.0%
2/18 – 2/23		CFFP MC Workbook	470	609	77.2%
2/24 – 2/28	1	Zahn Mock Exam	324	417	77.7%

ABOUT THE AUTHOR

Matthew Brandeburg is a Certified Financial Planner™ who runs his own financial advisory practice in Columbus, Ohio. Along with advising families and small businesses across the country, Matthew writes a weekly column for *Young Money Magazine* and is a nationally syndicated columnist for the *McClatchy-Tribune*. He is the author of the book *Financial Planning For Your First Job*, and has published over fifty personal finance articles in such publications as *Investment Advisor Magazine*, *The Journal of Financial Planning*, and *Business First*. In addition to writing, Matthew is a CFP® instructor at Ohio State University.

INDEX

Made in the USA
Charleston, SC
22 December 2010